GROWING UP

-

Dawta of JAH

Barbara Makeda Blake Hannah

GROWING UP – Dawta of JAH

Text (c) Barbara Makeda Blake Hannah

First published by Jamaica Media Productions Ltd. 2020

Jamaica Media Productions Ltd.,
P.O. Box 727, Kingston 6, Jamaica
jamediapro@hotmail.com

CONTENTS

INTRODUCTION

The first time I wrote about my life was in the biography *"GROWING OUT – Black Hair & Black Pride"* in which I told the story of my early years growing up as a schoolgirl in Jamaica, living as a young working woman, and then my move to England where I lived for 8 years and became – to my surprise – famous, as the first Black journalist to appear on British TV screens in the daily television programme *"Today With Eamonn Andrews".*

It was a story about how the racism I encountered in Britain – especially after getting that job – as well as the liberating and revolutionary thoughts of the 1960s, caused my evolution as a Black woman. It told how popular movements like the American "Black is Beautiful", the Black Panthers and Black Power, as well as the movements of Women's Liberation, Hippies, Anti-Vietnam War, mystic Indian philosophy, and especially the happy music and carefree lifestyle of Swinging London, all became a mixture of influences that eventually turned my face towards my native country, Jamaica.

Most influential of all in making this change in me from a devoted Black Englishwoman wishing my skin was white, my nose thin and my hair dead straight, into a Rastawoman growing out my natural dreads and loving my skin colour, was the film *"The Harder They Come"* that introduced me to the new Jamaica of Reggae and Rasta and had me trying to dance to the one-drop beat Toots & the Maytals *"Pressure Drop"*, while packing my suitcase for a happy return home to Jamaica.

The *'GROWING OUT'* biography ends there, with my farewell to England and my tribute to the many pleasures that I could hold as good memories to suppress the bad ones. I praised my friends Carol Martin-Sperry and fellow journalist- now-famous-author Celia Brayfield, restaurant owners Michael Chow and Robin Sutherland, comedians Peter Cook and Eric Idle, now-knighted theatrical director Richard Eyre, Olympic athlete Michael Palmer and the celebrated Oxford rowing coach Daniel Topolski.

I happily remembered such milestone events as the celebrity-filled opening party of the famous Kings Road restaurant-night club Trattoria Terrazza, and dinners at Knightsbridge's most famous restaurant Mister Chow, where my photo was on the wall with other show-biz celebrities, and where I enjoyed a white-wine-soaked farewell lunch with my beautiful Black American movie star girlfriend Vonetta McGhie, on vacation from her movie set at Rome's Cinicetta studios, and my beautiful Jewish-American girlfriend Rhea Goodman, fretting about her impending 40th birthday.

I was shocked and sad when Carol messaged me last week to say that Daniel had died of cancer. I found an obituary of him on the BBC website and was shocked to see how he had aged. The vibrant, handsome man who led Oxford University boat crew to 15 Regatta wins in a row and had a film made about him, was now a balding, white-haired man whom I could hardly recognize from the days when we drove madly around London in his open-top Mini Moke keeping up with his social life.

Tears welled, but remembering that Daniel was such a happy, lively person whose life I was glad to have shared, a big smile replaced them.

Time passes, and we all age. I looked back at the close of one half of my life, the England half, 50 years ago. The VOICE newspaper celebrated the anniversary in 2018 with a full-page article written by a young Black British journalist who said I was her inspiration.

Time to write the rest of the story now, Barbara, I told myself, holding back the tears. It will soon be your turn to leave and everyone wants to know what happened next, when you came home to spend the rest of your life in Jamaica.

As day broke, shedding its light into my bedroom, the computer kicked into life with its signature song. As my Facebook page opened up, a Friend had posted a picture of me being celebrated as a Black History Month icon by British magazine FashionFair UK.

The caption under the photo read:

"Before Moira and Trevor McDonald, there was Barbara Blake Hannah, Britain's first TV journalist, 1968."

I gave JAH thanks for seeing me, for showing me I was still remembered and my prayers heard.

Then I opened up this page and started writing.

BORN AGAIN

1972

I am a Bad Girl. Yes.
I am not a GOOD Girl.

A GOOD Girl would have come back from England and found herself a nice husband ... someone with brown-skin and 'good' hair (to keep the colour she inherited from her almost-white mother and straighten the children's noses), joined one of the Service Clubs – Rotary or Optimists or Friends of the British High Commission, or whatever ... and settled into Jamaica's middle and upper social classes ......

A GOOD Girl would have taken her father's advice and looked pleased that his old friend, that old senior civil servant with a title from the Queen, Sir Somebody Or Other, was interested in marrying a pretty young girl who would look after him patiently in his old age so she could inherit the house, the land and his wealth when he goes, and maybe have enough time left to catch a second husband before her looks were completely gone ....

Or, a GOOD Girl would have found herself a GOOD job, with some prestige and room for upward mobility, with a car and enough of a salary to merit a Mortgage for a House, or an Apartment – one of those TownHouses going up in New

Kingston or Barbican or even Cherry Gardens... no time for husband and children, but lots of high-profile charity work ...

Yes, a GOOD Girl would have done so many things.

But I am not a Good Girl.

I do not accept the normal.

I came back home to Jamaica in 1972 and rejected the normal.

I made a firm decision to accept no society-constructed barriers to my accumulation of knowledge and experience, but to freely explore the new world of Jamaica into which I had entered after a decade in Britain – the country my education and upbringing had trained me to enter, but which I had not found a comfortable fit because of the attitude of the residents to my colour and country of origin, and despite my well-meaning but historically stupid reason for seeing England as my 'Mother Country'.

Oh no, I was seeking a complete contrast to all that. I wanted to be different, to begin my new life as a Jamaican, like a new born babe, totally ignorant and uncaring of anything except the basics:

Eat,

Sleep,

Breathe,

Smile,

Be happy.

There were new roads to travel, new places to explore. Flowers to see, foods to eat, music to hear.

ALL OF JAMAICA to own as mine, my own, this

lovely, beautiful place.

I wanted to walk barefoot on the beach at night, again.

I wanted to play my guitar on a mountain balcony overlooking the city lights, again.

I wanted to dive with the dolphins and swim with fish, again.

I wanted to spend a day in a river and bathe in its waterfalls, again.

And I wanted to know who God is and if He knows that I exist.

* * *

I had a feeling that in Rastafari, I could find the answer to that quest.

I wanted, needed to know more about Rastafari.   It was a logical next stop on a personal development journey that had begun with living the musical and cultural revolution of the Swinging Sixties centered in London that combined the Eastern philosophies of the Hippies, the sexual freedom of the Womens Movement and, most expecially, the Black political revolution in which people like Angela Davis, Huey Newton, Malcolm X and Frantz Fanon were special heroes and influencers.

The Garveyist philosophy Rastafari taught was the natural political development for me of the Panthers "Black is Beautiful" philosophy, and I needed to know more about a movement that was speaking and acting and thinking this way in my own country.

So the choice I made to know more about and,

eventually, become a Rastafari, made me a Bad Girl in the opinions of Jamaica's moral judges, the people who decided who was 'accepted' and who was rejected from their circles. Thank heavens I had already decided to avoid those circles completely. They hadn't changed in my 10 years absence, only grown older.

The life I chose was far more interesting and, as time would eventually prove, fitted in completely with the Jamaica that was to bloom out of the Reggae Seventies. From the cultural enrichment of London's Swinging Sixties, I came home in 1972 at the birth of a musical and cultural movement that grows bigger and wider as years go by.

Within days of my return to Jamaica, I met the man who shone the brightest of reggae and Rastafari's musical and cultural lights around the world – Bob Marley. A small assignment put him in my life and he, his friends, his life and his religion were to become the most important experiences and life lessons of this Bad Girl.

In the Good Book Christ says: *"Ye must be born again to enter the Kingdom of Heaven."*

In 1972 – coming from England's cold weather and racism– Jamaica was the Kingdom of Heaven. I confessed my sins and considered myself Born Again.

LEARNING THE LANGUAGE

Standing on the verandah of my father's Port Antonio house, whose lawn faced the sea, with the sounds of waves crashing on the rocks beyond and the swish of breeze through the fir trees that bordered his yard, I was a Prodigal returning home.

It was a home in which I was a total stranger. I realised that even though I had lived the major part of my life in the country of my birth, I didn't really know it. Despite growing up as a child, then a teenager, then a young adult at the birth of Jamaica's Independence, I had an education that taught me more about England and Europe than Jamaica and Africa.

I knew more about the Wars of the Roses and Shakespeare and the climate of the Lake District, than I knew about the little island on which I was born. I had been well taught, well-trained in the Black Englishwoman brainwashing course known as a 'good' Jamaican high school education'. Hampton and Wolmers girls' schools may take credit.

Coming from 10 years of using that knowledge to earn a living in England, I was as uninformed about Jamaica as any foreigner would be. I even spoke like one, with the very 'proper' English accent with which I had made British history in 1968 as the first Black journalist to appear regularly on

British TV screens.

My accent gave me away, as I walked through the streets of Port Antonio, my little country hometown. My total ignorance of how things 'worked', how to buy food in the market, how to take a multi-person taxi, how to do anything the 'Jamaican' way, made me stand out as different.

I was a newborn baby. Innocent. Like a tourist visiting for the first time.

In ten years in England I had grown up from being a young girl into a young woman. I had lived in a strange country and absorbed its culture. I had understood it well enough to have achieved some small fame caused not just by my excellent absorption of the English culture, but because I seem to have achieved it because of, and in spite of, being Black.

But I hardly knew what being 'Black' was or meant. Having grown up accepting being part of a colour and race that was 'second class' in the world, learning to accept and even love that negative fact about myself, 'being Black' was something different and new. It was about recognising that 'being Black' was something to be proud of, something good – with a new history, a new knowledge and attitude to be learned.

I was a very new student in 1972.

So I decided to be my own kind of Good Girl, to be a new version of myself that I wanted to be, seeing and hearing and tasting and experiencing life through the Red, Gold and Green Spectacles of RasTafari.

"The Harder They Come" had propelled me towards Rastafari. I had been hired by Chris Blackwell to be PR in 1971 for the film's international launch at film festivals in Venice, Ireland and the British launch in Brixton. It was certainly a job where my colour and race were advantages. As Perry Henzell, the director, and his wife Sally - my friend from we both were 9 years old Hampton Girls school - took the film to festivals and screenings and press interviews, people were surprised that these persons behind the film were both White. It was stll a time when people thought that all Jamaicans were Black, but we Jamaicans knew that being Jamaican was not limited to being Black and this was especially visible in how accurately these White Jamaicans had portrayed the depths of Jamaica's Black culture in the film.

'The Harder They Come' became my introduction to Reggae and to Rastafari. The film showed a side of Jamaicam culture I had never known or experienced. I had not experienced the music of 'Downtown', under the social ban prohibiting 'well-brought-up' girls like me from listening or dancing to our own home-made sounds. These sounds had evolved and merged with a growing natonal awareness of our Black history into a beautiful cultural experience of sound and lifestyle. The music culture made Jamaica a strange country that had developed in the years I had been away. Jamaica was a place I did not know, with a language I did not speak. I was eager to know this new country and learn the language.

So I came home to Jamaica with a burning zeal to find out more about Rasta – what it was, what it meant, whether it was to be believed, or even lived. I had to know more. There was a scene in the film that generated my deepest curiosity: while a sweet song plays in the background, the hero rests in the shallows of a beach with a father and child playing happily, an iconic Rastaman with long, roots-like dreadlocks who is the warrior in the story's war against 'the system'. He rises up from the sea and flashes his locks up out of the water, sending a swoosh of spray exploding like a proud banner of a new alternative way of life declaring simplicity, morality and a belief in a new kind of God who is Black.

I had never seen anything that moved me quite like that strange sight of a different kind of man proudly declaring with his very different hairstyle a symbol of all those things. What it represented was a mystery to be explored because it intrigued me, it captured my mind in the empty space where belief in a God had been stirred since birth at many different spiritual stopping places, but never filled.

How to find it? All around me were the middle class people I knew and half-knew before I left Jamaica, a melting pot of colours and races firmly embedded in their elevated aspirations to live the cultural life left behind by the colonial masters – a life where Rasta culture was either something to be scorned or afraid of, except for those who would find places and spaces to hide and smoke ganja with Rastas around town, and around country. That life was not for me.

I had already experienced everything I was interested

in knowing about in my life so far, especially the decade in England meeting and moving among celebrities of fashion, film, music, media and revolutionary politics. I had lived the authentic high class life in Britain already, mixing with top people in the best of British society. My experience did not make me want more, much less to live its immitation in Jamaican attitudes, ideas and culture. I had found nothing yet as interesting, as intellectually and spiritually worth knowing more about, than Rastafari.

The Jamaican men I was meeting in the circles I was expected to move in, were all boring. Politics men were the topmost social level, even higher than Money men, which was a close second and often-times equal level of boredom. They all only talked about Politics. Or money. I couldn't find any of them attractive.

They were just simply Boring.

My girlfriend Beverly Anderson, with whom I had shared a London flat and many laughs in my first year before she returned to Jamaica, was now married to the biggest Politics man of all, the much-loved Prime Minister Michael Manley. Bev did her best to envelop me in her political social circle of the young men who had recently won the General Election and overthrown a very colonial-minded former government.

Michael Manley was the handsome, well-spoken, charimastic leader Jamaicans felt we deserved, a Third World political superstar among the new leaders of African countries that had recently gained independence from colonial masters, many of them with Cuba's help. When Michael spoke, making his points eloquently in a fiery manner that reminded all of Fidel Castro's revolutionary appeal, he inspired people to have hope his party could change Jamaica for the better. It sounded good coming from Michael.

I was told that Michael had used Rasta reggae artists in his round-the-island pre-election publicity tour and that it gave people hope that he would implement some Rasta-minded changes when he won. He had promised ganja law reform and people expected some echoes of Garveyism, Black Power and perhaps a little Rasta too when he came to power.

Rasta-minded people had even dreamed optimistically of Manley implementing the first steps of their dream of going back to Africa. So they were disappointed when Michael went to Cuba instead to visit Fidel Castro. Sadly, that was the start of the end of his Democratic Socialist dream to change Jamaica.

Such a pity.

The more I met and spoke with the politicians who ran the country, the less I could find of interest among them. I didn't hear any of the Marxist-Leninists around him saying anything that inspired me. There were definitely no Black Panthers among them, no Fidel Castros, no Mandelas, no Garveys. Just some people who read a German man's manifesto of how to organize the world without God, that they were trying to implement in Jamaica. Religion, they said he had said, was the opiate of the masses - whatever that meant.

I couldn't understand what Marxism-Leninism or Democratic Socialism were. No one could explain either in a practical way. There was little attempt to educate us in what these systems were anyway. These were just words. If you didn't know what those words meant, you were just one of the uneducated, illiterate 'lumpen proletariat', not included among the highly important political personalities running the government and the country. You were just 'voters' and 'crowd' to populate political meetings.

Still feeling like I was in a foreign country whose language I didn't speak, being around such people was truly boring.

I was more interested in the political potential of Rastafari's Afrocentric philosophy as a way to build the new Jamaica. But there was little instruction on how to get to know more about that philosophy.

So I struck out into the unknown.

I said to a Rasta man I met on the fringe of one of the political meetings: "I want to become a Rasta."

He looked at me to see if I was serious, then said: "I will take you to the teachers."

He drove me down to East Kingston, to Slip Dock Road off Windward Road where he picked up a man with a saxophone who he introduced as Tommy McCook. Then he drove further East up to Wareika Hill, to the Glasspole Avenue home of Brother Douggie Mack, my first Rasta teacher, who was to become the foundation of my knowledge of the history and livity of Rastafari.

Two houses away was the home and studio of the great Rastafari drummer Count Ossie, where Sam Clayton would 'teach' African history over the drumbeats of the Mystic Revelation of Rastafari.

We sat on stools among some men sitting in the shade of a zinc shelter at the back of Brother Dougie's house. He built me a spliff and as I lit it, Tommy McCook took up his saxophone and began to blow some of the sweetest music I had ever heard. The men around me smiled and made happy noises, one picked up an empty cooking pot and began beating a rhythm on the bottom, two others began to sing in harmony.

Thereupon began the happiest days of my life. Here, with the dirt of Brother Dougie's yard under my expensive London shoes and the smoke of the wood fire mixing with the smoke of ganja spliffs and chillum pipes being puffed by strange-looking men sitting all around me, I began my growing up as a Rasta.

I was so happy, I was smiling and smiling and smiling. Being in that backyard, so far away from everything and anything I had ever experienced in my life before, was simply the most wonderful experience of my entire life. It was a wonderful re-birth, the start of a new life in a Jamaica I had never known before, never even knew existed.

I feel that I was truly born again right there in 1972, a completely new person, given a chance to live my life all over again. A door had opened into a new world, and I was so very glad to be entering it, like an explorer finding a new civilization on a new planet.

My life began again in 1972 in Dougie Mack's yard. My frequent visits to Brother Dougie's home became the fountain of my knowledge, my education, and my development into the person I am today.

In the 1600s the explorer Ponce De Leon was told by the magicians at the Court in Spain to look for pools of Eternal life in the New World. These mystical crystal clear waters are known as Senotes in Guatemala and are scattered around an entire region known as the Devils Triangle, which I know is the JAH Triangle, a powerful portal in the earth where such natural pure watering holes are secreted. Bath Fountain in St. Thomas is one of those places.

Once I started walking the road of Rastafari, a very ital Brethren, Mihlawhdh Faristzaddi led me to a special Pool of Eternal Life at the Blue Lagoon in Portland. My little son Makonnen and I would bathe there often and the Pool rejuvenated me until I looked like a teenage girl, my body and even my mind refreshed.

The water there really was unusual, with red, yellow, green, blue, purple, orange flashes of prismatic lights. It was literally Crystal water. At first when I saw the lights I though it was the Ganja I was smoking, but when I sat and looked with the keen eye I did see the colours darting about from the silver light coming through the almond trees hanging overhead and skitting about in the water like small coloured fish. Only it was JAH light.

I had mystical experiences at that place. It was revealed that the source of the water goes down deep into the belly of the earth. It is a Keyhole Portal into Mother Earth. JAH set it there just for me.

The Pool has vanished now, disturbed and covered over by the building of expensive homes on the surrounding hillsides for residents to whom the pool was 'just more water'. I have a photo was taken at the pool when I was 47 years old. My son was 3. It's a very special photo and Mihlawhdh who took it says I look 20 years old.

That day in Dougie Mack's yard was my first dip in the Pool of Eternal Life.

It was 1972. Chronologically, I was 31 years old.

I am writing this in 2020, 79 years old.

People always tell me I look young for my age.

I was BORN AGAIN 48 years ago.

So I am 48 years old now.

48 Rasta Years young.

WAREIKA HILL - MY RASTA SCHOOL

I was never happier than those times I spent up at Wareika Hill in Brother Dougie Mack's back yard, around a fire, smoking ganja with Rastas and learning about my Black history. There was so much I didn't know. So much to learn. I was as innocent and as uneducated as a child. I knew nothing!

In Dougie Mack's back yard I was given 'The Philosophy and Opinions' of Marcus Mosiah Garvey to read.

I was educated about the Black origins of Egypt. I was told of the ancient Christian history of Ethiopia.

I learned the modern political history of Africa and its leaders.

I learned about Pan-Africanism, and how it existed long before Socialism.

I learned about the Black Heroes of African Liberation, yesterday and today, male and female.

I learned about the mysteries of the Constelations that stride through the skies at night.

Around that fire at night in Brother Dougie's back yard, with the drums of Count Ossie Mystic Revelation of Rastafari beating two yards away, I learned about the Black world I had been born into and lived most of my life in, without knowing anything of its true reality.

I had been taught White knowledge and White information and White ways of thinking to fit into a White world.

But now that I was learning a lot about my Black world that had been kept from me, I was learning about all that had been kept from my education as a Black person descended from enslaved Africans. I was beginning to see exactly what had caused that White world to be the awful world whose racism I had experienced so painfully. I began learning that the White world had done some awful things to my Black world and my Black people.

It was a terrible history to learn, with stories more shocking than anything I had ever heard. The atrocities of slavery and colonialism inflicted by Europeans, especially the English, made me wonder if White people were formed from the same flesh and blood as people like me. It made me wonder if people could be as cruel as White people were in the days of slavery.

And they still hadn't apologized and they still hadn't compensated us Black people for what they did and for the unpaid labour we Black people were forced to give them for three hundred years.

So why should I want to live in and be part of and think like that White world?

No way!

I was so glad I had left it and come home.

From now on I knew I would forever try to think with a Black mind and fill it with Black knowledge of ways of making my Black world better than the shocking state it was in now, because of what the White world did to it.

I learned that the massive displays of architectural and financial wealth I saw in London, Birmingham, Bristol, Manchester, Liverpool and other English cities had been built by the unpaid slave labour of my ancestors. Remembering the cities where I was considered an outsider with no right to breathe the air, but which had been made wealthy by the enslavement of my forefathers, I could see why Rastafari were calling for England to pay us Reparations out of the wealth our free work had given them then to build their great cities even to today.

I learned that I had a right to join the call by the children of those who were taken away from our continental homes, who insist they want to be returned to Africa in journeys paid for by the children of those who took us away. I learned about the call for Repatriation with Reparations.

Brother Dougie Mack had been one of four Rastafari brethren who were selected by Government to go on the first and second Missions to Africa, to see if any country was willing to accept Rastafari settlers. He came back and reported that they all were. But the Government did nothing with the Rasta report.

He was proud that when they met with the Ethiopian Emperor, Selassie invited them to remain in Ethiopia for several weeks. He still speaks about that special visit and has written a book "From Babylon to Rastafari" about it.

When Emperor Selassie came to Jamaica in 1966, Brother Dougie was one of the 12 persons to whom the Emperor presented a Gold medal. Brother Dougiw was a very special teacher.

But the BEST lesson I learned around that nightly fire from the wise men who sat in the dark beside their drums, was the Message of LOVE, the Message of the Christ, Iyesos Krystos, the Son of God. The men around the fire said the spirit of Christ had been born again in the person of His Imperial Majesty, Emperor Haile Selassie, King of Kings, Lord of Lords, Conquering Lion of the Tribe of Judah, Elect of God, Defender of the Holy Ethiopian Orthodox Faith.

They said he taught the Krystos message of Love. They said it was a new and precious message, but a difficult message to learn and to live. They said it was not about romantic love, hearts and flowers and that stuff. They said it was about having good feelings about all people, about everyone, no matter what. That was true LOVE.

I found it hard to believe. Yes, I could love the people I like, my friends, my family, people I meet, work with, things like that.

But how could I start to love White people – all White people -- when White people had made me hate them so much! White people had treated me so badly when I was living in England, hating me because of my colour.

If I had only known that it was THEY who should be hated for what they had done, I would have hated them even more.

I criticised myself for my ignorance.

But here were these men saying, No, that is not the way of Godliness. That is not the way of LOVE.

They said that LOVE was the opposite of HATE. They said that holding hate in my heart was not good for me. They said that Christ even said 'Turn the other cheek'.

You achieve more that way, they said. Send the message in the music, they said. Lick them with lyrics, they said.

Trust in the Christ we see in RAS TAFARI, Emperor Haile Selassie I, they said.

With the truths of my African origins and the generations of my ancestors who had suffered in slavery revealed to me in stark and unending detail, I was at the same time being taught that the revenge for it all should not be hatred and vengeance, but that I should strive to live my life better without evil, without doing bad things, being BETTER than those who had oppressed, brutalized and murdered me and people like us.

Be like Christ, they said.

It was a lot to accept and believe.

I knew about Christ ... I had been baptized a Catholic as a baby at Holy Rosary Church, Windward Road. As we grew up, my sister and I were sent to the imposing and historic Coke Methodist Church in the downtown West Parade on Sunday mornings. I was confirmed an Anglican at Hampton boarding school in St. Elizabeth, aged 14. I stood up for Billy Graham at his massive public meeting at Knutsford

Park, Kingston, aged 17 and shouted with the crowd "Yes, I sincerely want to be saved!" I made myself dresses to wear to church at St. Luke's Anglican Church, Cross Roads on Sundays, as I reached my 20s. And I still considered myself a 'Christian' even though I eventually stopped going to church in Jamaica and never went in England.

But this Rasta interpretation of a modern-day Christ was definitely not the same as the one I had been taught through all those years. The Christ these Rastas wanted me to believe in they said was reborn in a man that was alive on the Earth, a re-incarnation in these times of the same Christ we read about in the Bible, who was crucified, died on a cross and was born again three days later.

How could that be?

It was hard to believe, yet it was the foundation of their beliefs.

They challenged me to deeply consider that people have forgotten what the first manifestation of God in Man came to teach us, how to think and how to be Christly, how to LOVE. They said it was clear that two thousand years after that first manifestation of Christ came as Jesus of Nazareth, people are not behaving like the example JAH sent to Earth.

So they explained that JAH felt it was time to send another Manifestation, in the form of Emperor Haile Selassie the First, King of Kings, Lord of Lords, Elect of God, Conquering Lion of the Tribe of Judah, Defender of the Faith, as the Returned Messiah, the man with all the titles, the man who lived a perfect life, the man whose coming would restore

Heaven on Earth.

Peace and Love must come on Earth, they said.

It had come with H.I.M. to us, they said.

We are here to spread it to the world, they said.

*

It took many years for me to learn, to OVERstand what the men around Dougie Mack's fire saw in H.I.M. It took me years to see with a heart and mind like theirs, how a man we could only see in pictures and whose life and speeches we could only read about, was a man who had lived a life that was a very pure and shining example of a CHRISTly life that I could follow.

I learned to overstand how Rastafari see the CHRISTLY-ness of Haile Selassie I.

Looking at the world today, it is clear that 2000 years after Jesus of Nazareth was sent by God to show Mankind how to think and be and live, Mankind has forgotten the real example that was sent. We are no longer following that example. Mankind has become the opposite of what Jesus of Nazareth stood for. We have replaced LOVE with Hate and PEACE with War.

Who can believe that the people who make brutal war against each other, who commit sexual immorality of all kinds, who value money higher than righteousness, who raise children without teaching them about God, can possibly be seen as living examples of the first Christ?

Today, in our time, Rastafari have seen a living example of the Perfect Man that Jesus of Nazareth was described to be, a human example born in the holiest country in Africa, descended from the holiest Biblical lineage, honoured by Church and by innumerable international States and statesmen. Rastafari therefore hold that man in divinely high regard.

This man has inspired me to try and be like CHRIST. To be CHRISTly.

I am still trying to achieve that objective. Knowing how much of a failure I am at it, I am consoled by the fact that JAH rewards honest effort and sincere faith, so I therefore keep trying.

Since those early leasons in the African CHRISTianity of Rastafari beliefs, my knowledge of Christ has been expanded by learning about and living the teachings of the Ethiopian Orthodox Tewahedo Church, of which Emperor Haile Selassie wore the title Defender of the Faith.

I learned this wisdom in the Wareika Hills around Brother Dougie Mack's fire. By accepting these truths, I slowly began to think and act and live as RASTA.

It was the start of a process of 'becoming Black' that had begun in England as a reaction to racism, and which continued flourishing now in the fertile Black cultural garden of Eden, Jamaica.

COMMUNITY SERVICE

My visits to Dougie Mack's yard and Count Ossie's cultural events became my education in becoming an African-minded, Africa-focused, Africa-visioned Jamaican, and a Rasta.

I stayed connected to Wareika Hill a lot in my first years back home in Jamaica. I had a job as a journalist on a new daily newspaper, the Jamaica Daily News, that had just started publishing, and a small apartment in New Kingston with a pool in the backyard and plenty of time on my hands, so I would go and spend time with Bro. Dougie and his family and absorb the cultural activities that were always happening at Count Ossie's yard.

Realising over time how much the children and youths I was getting to know admired and were curious about me and why I was so different, I started a youth club – the Wareika Association of Youths (the WAY, we called it) to see if I could add something to the lives of the young people of the hillside community. We met weekly, played games, talked about history or current affairs, school and education and what they hoped life would be, and generally enjoyed having a good reason to be out socialising away from parental supervision one evening a week.

It was an interesting group of Kingston youths, the

youngest being 'Bobby Reds' who boasted "I am 13 an' me have FOUR baby mothers". I couldn't believe him, but it turned out it was true. Another of the girls was 15 and had twins, already a teenage mother like most of the girls would become.

There was Paul, who had bad headaches that caused him constant distress and made people say he was 'mad', but he was a quiet leader especially when there was strife between any of them. None of them had a 'real' job or a proper education, but all shared hopes of escaping the poor situations in which they lived. My job was to encourage them to keep trying.

I enjoyed being with them and sharing my views and experiences. Once a week I would take the bus from home to the main road close to Wareika Hill and then walk through the community till I reached the small schoolhouse that served as our 'clubhouse'. People thought I should have been afraid walking through 'the ghetto', but I remembered the neighbourhood from years ago before I left Jamaica when it was a nice, middle-class community of homes, so I never was afraid. In any case, the youths would walk me back to the bus stop when the evening was over. No trouble.

Once I told Mr. Carlton Alexander, a very important Jamaican businessman I met in my job, about the club and the youths and invited him to come, not thinking he would. To my great surprise, he called one night to say his driver was picking me to up to take us both to that night's meeting! How could I refuse?

It was a tight fit for the gentleman to squeeze his large body in the half-broken desk-and-chair that was all the furniture in the small room, and the children were astonished to see that someone so important, and so White, had actually come over into their ghetto to spend an evening with them, but he just made a joke of it.

I made each of them stand and say who they were and what they wanted to with their lives. Then I had him tell them who he was and what he believed in life. They asked him questions about all sorts of things, but they never begged him any money. The gentleman was a real gentleman and it was a very special evening.

We held a Christmas Eve Fair that year, where the youths got neighbourhood shops to contribute small toys and presents to keep a party for the children. When I told him about it, Mr. Alexander, who was actually the boss of a major food distribution company -- sent us some cases of his company's products and money to buy cake, ice cream, drinks and a goat. We served curry goat and rice to all the children and their parents on Wareika Hill that Christmas Eve night. We had a great time!

I continued my links with Wareika Hill for many years. Sadly, activities on Glasspole Avenue weakened and finally came to an end when Count Ossie died in a car accident after a performance by MRR at the National Stadium on Heroes Day. The heart and spirit went out of us all with the drummer's missing beat. No one could play the drums like Count Ossie. He was one of a kind and though many have come close, no one has yet been as flexible, as musical, as powerful on the drums as he was.

Worse, 'politics' came into play in East Kingston and the area became very politicized. Some of the youths went to Cuba to be trained as 'Brigadistas' and came home fine-tuned political soldiers, hotting up the fight to keep the Constituency in PNP control.

Robin Hood-style ghetto warriors like 'Copper' took survival tactics to a new level with daring bank robberies in which he escaped by throwing money behind him as the motor bike he was carrried on sped through the narrow Wareika Hill streets, with the residents pointing the pursuing Police in the other direction. It was urban guerilla war, and Wareika Hill became even more dangerous.

Dougie Mack moved to America with his wife and daughters, and still lives there. I was sad to see him go, and I was glad to see him again when he last visited Jamaica a few years ago. I am still his faithful student. I keep contact with Count Ossie's son and daughter, and used to visit Brother Sam Clayton often in his old age, before he died recently.

The history, the music and memories will live on of the great days when Wareika Hill was the cultural centre of Jamaica and of Rastafari.

BECOMING A RASTAWOMAN

I was fortunate to be a young woman at the start of the Sexual Revolution, that era of the 1960s when the discovery of the contraceptive pill coincided with the literary and verbal expressions of some bold women who dared to speak out about their feelings, lives and – especially – their sex lives. Their bold look at what a woman could do in this enlightened age, allowed us to consider new extensions to the boundaries that had hitherto fenced female behaviour In previous years.

I lived in England during those pioneering years and 'Swinging London' was a center of the new world of 'feminism'. Germaine Greer, the Australian icon of the Swinging Sixties counter-culture wrote *"The Female Eunuch"*, a best-seller embraced by millions of women around the world as guide to their expression of female self-hood. She was one of my friends and I embraced her ideas of female liberation as part of my own racial liberation, which was guided just as influentially by another female icon – Black American Angela Davis.

With the freedoms that had become my norm thanks to both women, becoming a RastaWOMAN living and behaving as women of my community were supposed to was a new learning process, some of which directly opposed the teachings I had so happily accepted as a 'feminist'. But just as

I had left England completely to follow a way of life completely different from the life I had previously lived, I was prepared to do whatever was necessary to be accepted as a student traveller along the Rastafari pathway.

In started obeying the Rastafari dress code for women from the top. Though I didn't start off by growing locks and continued combing out my hair, I covered my head with a colourful headwrap every where. I selected bright and beautiful wraps in different colours and tied up my hair in them daily.

In the beginning people were unwilling to accept women displaying this fashion, as it identified a woman following the Rastafari lifestyle. It stopped my chances of getting many jobs, and I combed it out into an Afro years later to get a job as Director of PR for the City of Kingston.

But as time pased, covering my hair became acceptedk especialy when my locks grew and grew longer and looked so pretty. I still cover my head every day, as I am an Empress and my headcovering is my 'crown'.

Clothing was another part of the dress code. 'Sexy' clothes that displayed the breasts, curves of hips and buttocks, even bare shoulders, were not allowed. We 'queens' did not wish to 'rise up the sap' in strange men as we pass by in public. Funnily enough, covering often made us even more attractive!

Most important of all was the ban on trousers. I learned that the hard way on my first visit to a Nyabinghi celebration. The Rastaman I was living with took me there.

I wore a pair of beautiful, well cut green velvet trousers I had purchased in Cannes while working for the BBC at the famous film festival. I had a lot of trousers in my wardrobe, because I was very self-conscious about what I considered my very skinny legs. This pair was my favourite and I had another identical pair in navy blue velvet.

As we entered the tabernacle, an Elder Rastaman with thick gray locks flowing from under a big tam, leaped up from his seat on a bench inside and, gesticulating with a chalice in one hand, started shouting abusively at me.

"Who you think you are, coming in here dressed like a man? Are you the Queen Lie-Za-Bed that rules England? You are an insult to your race and to your Sisterhood! Get out of here!!!"

I was shocked breathless, like a bullet had hit me. I rushed outside, got in the car and begged to be taken home immediately. My man agreed to take me home, but only to change into a skirt, he said. If I didn't do that and return to the Nyabinghi, I would forever regret it. Didn't I say I wanted to be a Rasta?

When we got home he took up his Bible and showed me where it was written that a woman should not wear man's clothing and that a woman's head should be covered when she prays. He reminded me that in Africa most women wear skirts or wraps, and African tribes-women don't wear trousers.

He reasoned with me that trousers show too much of the outlines of a woman's private parts and legs that should only be seen by her partner. He told me that skirts provided the modesty a woman should have, and said that modesty in a woman was very attractive to a man, especially to a man looking for a 'good' woman as his partner and mother of his children.

I took a while to consider, but as he reminded me, I had returned to Jamaica TO BECOME A RASTA. Rasta women don't wear men's clothing, he said.

With a sigh, I found a hardly-worn dress in my wardrobe, put it on and very shyly returned to the 'Bnghi' yard, hoping to be un-noticed in the crowd.

No such luck.

The same booming voice was coming out from the same Elder dread.

"Ah, you come back! Welcome my beautiful Princess!! Come sit right here beside me and tell me all about you'self!!"

"Whe' you come from? You come outta Babylon? You just reach? Welcome! WELCOME!"

He handed me a handful of herb and a piece of corn trash to roll it in and made other people move down on the bench to give me a seat beside himself, smiling with a grin missing several teeth.

I was astonished. Speechless.

My man just smiled and stepped back into the crowd that was also full of smiling faces.

I sat there for hours with the Elder, who I grew to know well over the years as Bongo Daniel. He handed me a little calabash shaker and I just sat there happily shaking the shaker, smoking spliff after spliff, listening to the singing and harmonising and drumming surrounding me in a cloud of LOVE.

"So be wise and step inside, and do not be like some of them who throw their lovely chances away."

So sang the Nyabinghi choir.

I felt I had arrived home at last. Just by wearing a skirt. I haven't work a pair of trousers since that night in 1973.

I found that men love skirts.

They love the mystery.

They love long skirts that fit around the hips.

They love floaty skirts that ripple in the wind.

They love to see a woman sweep up her skirt to walk, or sit, or move

Nowadays, when so few women wear skirts any more, a woman in a beautiful skirt always gets a second look.

You see, men wear trousers. So there's no mystery when women wear them, especially those trousers nowadays, they call them 'tights', that show their curves and all there is to give and especially, the places to receive.

But skirts ... men's imaginations can go wild.

So men say.

No RastaWOMAN can claim to be the best or only representative of the Sisterhood. But many blessed Sisters, Pricesses, Queens and Empresses will humbly bow their heads to be counted among the Royal Assembly.

GARVEY'S BLACK PHILOSOPHY

It was Marcus Garvey who first showed me the road to Rastafari. A few weeks after I returned to Jamaica in 1972, I attended an event at the Sheraton Kingston Hotel to hear a speech by Evonne Goolagong, an Australian half-Aboriginee girl who had just won Wimbledon. I did not know that whatever admiration I had for this great tennis player who had just made Black history, would pale by comparison with the eye-opening shock of hearing a frail, 82-year old woman speak in a commanding and excited voice about a true Black Hero whose life and philosophy she demanded that we follow. She was Mrs. Amy Jacques Garvey and the man she spoke of was her husband Marcus Mosiah Garvey.

I had never heard of Marcus Garvey before that day. My education in Black History had begun only a few years earlier in England, where racism made me absorb all the "Black is beautiful" information then being spread by American activists of the Black Power movement. I knew about Martin and Malcolm and even Elijah Muhammad, but not Marcus, so it was electrifying for me to hear this small, but fiery woman speak passionately about what Marcus Garvey stood for – the mental as well as physical liberation of the Black mind.

This woman's words forced me to read the book she published of Garvey's '*Philososphy and Opinions*' and in it I found how beautifully they contributed to the information necessary for my full mental liberation from slavery.

Of course, stepping onto the path of Garvey knowledge was the best place to encounter Rastafari – the people who Garvey's words had inspired to not only seek to return to the African Motherland from which their ancestors had been taken, but even more importantly, to see Black Divinity in a Crowned African Emperor whose dynasty stretched back in ecclesiastical history to Solomon, the Queen of Sheba, David and Jerusalem - H.I.M. Emperor Haile Selassie.

I thus continued to travel the Rastafari pathway, seeking knowledge to add to my racial emancipation. I found the best interpretation of Garvey's teachings among the Rastafari elders, the true and most faithful keepers of Marcus Garvey's flame. In true Garveyite principle, Rastafari saw Garvey as the Prophet who pointed Black people in the West to their African homeland. Rastafari were always the most visible and outspoken Jamaicans speaking out about Garvey at all celebrations and events, flying the Black, Red and Green banner of the UNIA next to the Ethiopian Red, Gold and Green. I found Garvey depicted in RASTA iconography, along with Emperor Haile Selassie and EAIBC Priest Prince Emanuel, as the Holy Trinity.

The relationship between Garvey and Rasta has not

always been a smooth one. There was a recent time when the UNIA and Rastafari were not close, each side quoting Garvey's condemnation of Emperor Selassie for leaving Ethiopia for asylum in England from the Italian invasion, as reasons why they did not get along with the other group.

Those days are far gone, as a dreadlocksed, professed Rastafarian – Stephen Golding – is now leader of the Jamaican UNIA. Garvey has become respected by the 'middle classes' and even more RASpected than ever by the Rastafari masses who always followed his teachings.

As for those not of Garvey's race or mindset who are still uncomfortable about Garvey's sole focus on race – some even terming it 'Black racism' – the 'race' puss is well out of the bag, thanks more to a reflection of the gains of the US civil rights movements then and now against racism, than the efforts by the UNIA at home and abroad. I am certain that many still think it's dangerous to teach Black people to take hold of their destiny based solely on their Blackness, but their views are a minority that gets smaller as a new multi-ethnic generation grows up.

The fight to teach Garvey in Jamaican schools as not just a figure in history but by sharing his Black philosophy, has not yet been won. It would clearly need a complete re-order of the Jamaican 'System', based on Garvey's teachings for that to be achieved. World History would begin in Egypt, not Greece and instead of the Middle Ages, would focus on Africa and the growth and under-development of the

Caribbean through the Slave Trade.

Mathematics would be part of a Science curriculum including Engineering and teaching of the Arts and Literature would be practical, hands-on performances and written work, as Garvey did with his publications and events at Liberty Hall. Teaching of Business Management would begin at Primary level, producing graduates with practical experience to provide Africa with trained development specialists in several fields and providing the home nation with economic and trade alliances with other Black nations and people.

Potential Jamaican leaders often tiptoe around the matter of Race (with a capital 'R'), pretending it is invisible when 99% of the crowd is African-descended. An enlightened leadership could use Garvey as the captain to steer the ship of State into prosperous waters, with wise communication programmes in which race becomes regarded as a quality of pride on which to restore a nation and people, instead of still being regarded as a negative – despite all the words and hard work of Mr. Marcus Mosiah Garvey.

Mrs. Amy Jacques Garvey so inspired me to spread the words of Marcus Garvey, that in 1972 I made it a personal commitment to start writing articles about Garvey and his philosophy. Each year on his Birthday I would send a Letter to the GLEANER Editor (then Hector Wynter) that would usually be that paper's only or main memorial.

In 1981, while doing some voluntary PR service for the

UNIA, I proposed to the Minister of Foreign Affairs (then Hon. Dudley Thompson) that the Ministry building be re-named the Marcus Garvey Building. He accepted and the name still stands on what is now the Courtleigh Hotel, New Kingston.

In 1986, while serving as an Independent Opposition Senator in the Jamaican Parliament, in my first Debate I proposed that the upcoming Centenary of the birth of Hon. Marcus Garvey be celebrated as a National holiday. The Government Senators, led by then-Minister of Culture Olivia Grange, voted against the proposal, saying the country could not afford a national holiday, granting instead a holiday in St. Ann - the Parish of Garvey's birth. I accepted that. I had made my point.

My favourite Garvey link of all, was being put in charge of the activities surrounding the 1975 unveiling of Garvey's statue at the St. Ann Parish Library. Working at the time as assistant to the Culture Minister in the Office of the Prime Minister, I monitored the arrival in Jamaica of the statue, its transportation to St. Ann and the building of a cutstone pedestal and wall in front of the Parish Library.

My special action was to find a way to cover the statue before the unveiling, so I got a dressmaker to add a stripe of red fabric to a huge Jamaican flag, used it to cover the huge statue and tied it with a special rope in a way to unveil it in one tug.

It was a sunny day and bright afternoon, with music performed by Count Ossie's Mystic Revelation of Rastafari giving the gathered crowd the right vibrations. But as soon as the official ceremony began Mr. Garvey decided to attend 'in the whirlwind and the storm' and a sudden and thunderous downpour swamped the event with rain falling in buckets. As the Prime Minister and special guests crowded around the statue in the pouring rain, the flag drape became waterlogged.

I stepped forward to help the PM find the rope tug, but even though I had worked hard to make it all happen, my boss the Minister of Culture pushed me away from the statue when he saw I was wearing a skirt of red, gold and green colours. As the rain poured down, Manley tried and tried and failed to find a way to pull the flag off the statue. I just stood under shelter and watched them all get soaking wet, until someone finally just ripped the wet cloth off.

There is no photographic record of that historic unveiling. The downpour was so great that none of the photographers could raise their cameras, so the deluge prevented any photographs from capturing the actual unveiling by Michael Manley. Read into that what you will. I could see Mr. Garvey in everything that happened.

These have been some of the ways in which I have sought to pay tribute to the freeing of my mind by Mr. Garvey's philosophy and the teachings that revised my thinking about myself as a Black person and made me proud for the first time to be Black. Garvey's words gave me a motivation for my future focus and work, and they confirmed that my choice of Rastafari as my life and spiritual pathway is appropriate and totally in keeping with what Mr. Garvey taught.

In 2018 the UNIA Jamaica presented me with a Lifetime Achievement Award, of which I am extremely proud.

I think Mr. Garvey would have been proud to meet me. I, of course, will be BLESSED to meet him one day in Zion.

BOB MARLEY – A FRIEND I USED TO KNOW

Bob Marley was a remarkable Black man, the kind that occurs unfortunately too infrequently in the history of the African Diaspora. Speaking as a Black Woman, there are so few who represent the free Black man -- not slave -- that when we meet one we must pause to reflect on just how truly great a Black man can be.

I made my first visit to 56 Hope Road in 1972 just after returning from living in England, where my last job was doing the PR for the international launch of Chris Blackwell and Perry Henzell's film *"The Harder They Come"*. Bob had just been signed to Island Rcords to produce the first, sensational album *'Catch A Fire'* and Blackwell asked me to show some American journalists around Kingston and to meet the new artists he had just signed. That was Bob Marley and from that day's introduction I became a friend.

He and the Wailers were sitting like wet chickens on the steps leading to ther apartment upstairs the garage of 56 Hope Road, which was then their headquarters for many months before they moved into the big house in front.

Though they seemed out of place and ill at ease in their surroundings, the fire of their spirit and their rebellious anger smouldered behind their quiet faces. Bob was an unforgettable personality. I did my job showing the journalists around Kingston, then continued on my urgent, personal quest to discover and become Rastafari, but I was able to watch Bob evolve from those early days..

In 1974 I met the Wailers again while I was organizing the first Jamaica Film Festival and on the recommendation of my advisors, tried to hire the Wailers to perform at our Awards ceremony. Though our budget did not allow us to hire them eventually, my friendship continued with Bob and his brethren. I argued in print the Wailers right to their first big fee on the Jackson Five Show, when a late start caused the Jacksons to perform first and Bob and the Wailers then entertained a packed Stadium crowd till four in the morning.

And like many others, I hung around 56 Hope Road whenever I could just to be among the peaceful, beautiful vibrations of Rastafari that encircled everyone radiating from Bob's center. When I worked at the Office of the Prime Minister that was just within walking distance, I would stop there on my way home and soak up the Rasta energy that filled the space. Bob's brethren milled around the yard, visitors came and went, music was always playing. It was a constant spectacle full of LOVEing vibrations.

Bob came to consider me a good friend and I was close enough to have been in the studio one day when he was recording *"I'm A Black Survivor"* with his wife Rita. At one point Bob took a break, sat down on the floor beside a stool I was sitting on and fell asleep. I was surprised, but felt very honoured that he was comfortable enough with me to do that.

Someone woke him up out of the nap and when he

jumped up, I felt like a little lion had leapt out of my lap. Bob's spirit? Who knows.

I was never a girlfriend though, and I knew that Bob had many affairs. One Saturday afternoon he and his best friend Allan 'Skill' Cole stopped by my flat and did their best to persuade me and a girlfriend to accompany them to Cane River Falls, where they would go regularly to wash their locks and enjoy some time in the wild river valley. But I was afraid of the intimacy that I knew would follow if I accompanied them, so I turned down the offer. In any case, I already had a man.

But as I was now growing as a Rasta, I and friends like myself enjoyed being around Bob and the new musical experience that was happening with him as its chief guru. It was very good for my education as a Rasta to be among all the irie friends who hung around the old Hope Road mansion in the early years. Those were good times when Bob would relax by strumming his guitar under the ackee tree in the backyard.

I remember one evening when Bob and his bredrin were reasoning with some fragrant cool herbs and enjoying life. Bob just picked up his guitar and said to Dermot Hussey, the host of a popular radio programme: "Hear some new songs I'm working on..." and just started to play, song after song, music after music, some complete, some just snatches, music flowing out of Bob like pure water flowing from a river.

When we all just listened and marvelled in quiet admiration, then praise, but Bob just smiled and shrugged off the praise saying: *"Not I, but the Most High in I"*.

It's a phrase I've never forgotten and used often since then, because it says exactly where anything worth praising comes from. I don't know which songs they were, or if any of them ever became songs we know. But it was just a very special moment as the dusk shadows dropped on a beautiful Rasta evening.

Sometimes Bob would kick some ball on the front lawn that was now a dusty yard because of all the times Bob kicked ball there. There would be maybe five or six other friends playing, usually Skill Cole among them, but Bob was a one-man team, everybody else was the other team and his team mus' win. Bob played hard and it was fun to watch him playing. Everyone would be laughing, watching him play.

It was like being in the presence of a Holy Man, yet Bob had no airs and never changed from being just a down-to-earth, feet-in-the-dust man -- Christ-like, is the analogy that comes to mind.

It wasn't always easy for me to keep visiting, as the business grew and became formalized and managers became over-protective, but I continued to stop by whenever I could. Moreover, as woman, Rasta-woman, African-woman -- a friends-only relationship is a finely-balanced and delicate entity, preserved only by discretion and respect.

As he became more famous and, especially after the attempted murder before the 'Smile Jamaica' concert. I got to see that concert from the stage through some amazing good luck. I had been standing at the bus stop on Lady Musgrave Road waiting to go by muself to Heroes Park, when Prime

Minister Michael Manley passed by with his many-car Police entourage. He stopped the cars and offered me a lift, and that is how I went with him and his bodyguards, family and friends onto the stage and watched history unfold. After that show, when the dangers of Bob's existence became obvious, the casual moments around Bob became fewer, but Bob was always glad to see me.

There was the afternoon when I came to tell him that my proposal the he be given the Keys to the City had been turned down by the then-City Fathers. Bob just shrugged and said "Never mind, I only said Yes because it was you who asked me, Barbara. Babylon mus' burn!"

For Bob was accustomed to rejection from an administration whose highest house of culture -- the Institute of Jamaica -- had never seen fit to award him an honour, not even when they gave out 500 Centenary Medals. Bob - a prophet without honour in his own country until he lay on his deathbed.

It was the last time I saw Bob. He had some visitors, a famous Black American musician who was in awe of meeting Bob, (I forget his name). Then he played some football, Bob as usual against the rest of the men on the field, and Bob as usual the BEST player on the field. Then he sat down to rest and read from the autobiography of Emperor Haile Selassie.

"You read this yet, Barbara?" he asked. I had not. "What?" he was astonished, but smiling. "You fi read it, Sis. Knowledge and wisdom in dis book!" When I eventually said I had to leave, he called someone and told him to drive me home. "Carry her whichever part she wan' go!" were his instructions to the man ,and the last words I heard from Bob.

Bob attracted by being a warrior for the cause of Justice and the rights of the still-poor children of slaves. This gave him an aura more powerful than that which is based on popular fame or sensuality, for it created Perfect Love between Bob and the millions in tune with his Divine Vibrations.

These vibrations emanated from his songs which touched chords in the hearts, memories and wombs of us Black women, lyrics which we could only feel but not express as we -- from a distance, from a memory stretching back through our mother's mother -- remembered the pain we had suffered when our fathers, daughters, sons and lovers were taken from us, as we worked endlessly for No Pay, Low Pay, Lie Down Pay, Suck Salt Pay. As we took on the beauty standards of another race's women in an attempt to win the favour of our masters, and those of our men who loved our master's women.

Like Garvey before him, Bob helped us free ourselves from those pains and replace them with the joys of being a part of a New Creation of Black Madonnas, of a new African-ness, cleansed with a new vision, a wider breadth and a richer strength. That vision encompassed a view of a Black warrior, bearing not a spear or a gun, but the peaceful music of Love -- Love of Black Man, Love of Black Woman, Love of Black People and Love of All People. The Prince of Peace, the total Rastaman.

Who could help loving him, who heard his Psalms of Love, Righteousness and the inevitability of Black Redemption. Only the wicked hated him, for his words made them uneasy and they feared the sight of his locks, the mark of warrior which he wore like the Mau Mau of Kenya before him. And like them, he too was a guerilla warrior, but his weapons were the words of his songs -- hatred of downpression, anger at poverty, the injustice of slavery, the need for Repatriation (whether actual or simply cultural and spiritual), the love of GodJAH and the recognition of one's Divine Spirit.

In his last year, Bob's spiritual emphasis broadened to include Garvey and Christ, even being baptized in the Ethiopian Orthodox Church in the name of Christ. "Africa in ten years time? Africa will be dreadlocks -- Christ's Government will rule," he said in an interview broadcast on the day of his death.

Yes, JAH would never give the power to a baldhead, and the message had come instead in the sweetest, Blackest and most divine form -- words of song from a man who had experienced the Christ example through a Black King on an African throne. And though we may crucify the dread, time alone will tell that it was not wrong to see the Conquering Lion of the Tribe of Judah as the Christ reborn for the Black Man and Woman today. For in seeing H.I.M., a lot of people tried to live Life right, in a Christly way, in the name of JAH RASTAFARI.

Bob was human also, flesh with weaknesses like

David, who he was in another incarnation. But whatever his fleshy weaknesses, they are in the dust, while Bob's message is everliving, continuing for years and years and years.

And the message Bob lived, sang and died to show us was the truths of Marcus Garvey, Haile Selassie and Iyesos Christ in an African way, for all the peaceful Black warriors of today, and for all Mankind. For Ethiopia shall truly stretch forth her hands unto God, and we are the Ethiopians.

Peace & Love, Bob. You have earned your place in Zion.

A BRIEF MOMENT WITH FIDEL CASTRO

One shining moment of the Socialist Seventies was the visit to Jamaica of Cuba's revolutionary leader Fidel Castro, who spent five days being shown around a cheering island accompanied by a large retinue and motorcade of Cuban bodyguards and PNP faithful. All Jamaica was delighted, for Fidel was a hero to us all, especially because of his help to the many African nations fighting colonialism, and especially his help to South Africa.

The trip was almost a one-week national holiday with crowds gathering along highways and at Fidel's stops, finally culminating in a well-attended press conference at Kingston's largest hotel. I made sure to be there as it would be my only opportuniy to see the great man in person. He was someone I admired greatly for how he had overthrown American colonialism and made Cuba a new country, but most of all for how he had led Cuba and Cuban soldiers to help so many African liberation wars.

I was certainly not an official member of the 'press', but I was a journalist and I had a question for my hero Fidel.

I waited until the crop of established journalists had run out of questions, before stepping to the microphone with my hand raised. One PNP official at the head table who knew me well as an 'outsider' tried to wave me down, but I ignored him and looked Fidel in the eyes.

"You once said that one day Cubans will no longer work for money, but people will work instead only for the good they do and the good they receive. When will Cuba reach that stage?" I asked.

Fidel looked surprised and raised his eyebrows at my question, looking me straight in the eyes while listening to the translation of my words, then he smiled and answered in Spanish: "Thank you for your question Companera. Cuba is still working towards that day, but we looked around and saw so many people who needed Cuba's help that we had to stop working in our own interests and help them," he replied.

As he noticed me nodding in overstanding of his Spanish before the interpreter's English translation, he spoke faster and more directly to me.

"This is what we have been doing in Africa for several years in several countries, helping our brothers and sisters fight the colonial liberation wars that we were better able and equipped to do, and although we are criticized for doing that, Cuba will continue helping our brothers and sisters as long as we can."

Mine was the last question and the officials wrapped up the press conference. Everyone exited the room and crowded in the lobby around Fidel as he waited for the lift. I stood six feet away from Fidel as he waited surrounded by his people, Jamaican officials and the press. But as we all stood waiting, he kept looking at me, looking into my eyes, until the lift finally opened and he turned and stepped inside.

As I was leaving the hotel, a small bunch of Cuban officials rushed past me on their way to the cars. One of them, a red-haired white man, slowed down, smiled and said to me in Spanish: "Fidel liked your question best."

Who was that, I asked a PNP person.

"The Cuban Director General of Intelligence," he replied.

HOLLYWOOD & BLACKSPLOITATION

I have organized a lot of film festivals. Eleven, to be exact. I never planned to have 'film festival organizer' on my resume, but after a visit to Hollywood in 1974, here's how the first one happened.

While living in London I had met Vonetta McGee, a very, very beautiful light-brown-skinned Black American Hollywood movie star who was acting in 'spaghetti Westerns' in Rome's film studios when I met her. We became good friends and twice she came to London on holiday and stayed with me in my tiny Notting Hill Gate flat.

Vonetta was born for Hollywood. The Dorothy Dandridge of her time and an early Halle Berry, she knew how to be a 'movie star'. She could act well enough, but it was her astonishing beauty and a happy, witty personality that charmed everyone who met her and made her a perfect Hollywood star.

Developing her career by acting in the Italian 'spaghetti westerns', she made a big impact with her role in Sergio Corbucci's classic Italian Western *"Il Gran Silencio"* (*"The Big Silence")* that gave her international impact.

Vonetta had the right experience when the 1970's 'Blacksploitation' films with Black stories and actors started being made in Hollywood and rapidly became popular, films like "The Mack" and "Shaft". The films were called 'Blacksploitation" because some people felt they exploited Black people by featuring caricature Black roles – pimps, prostitutes, gangsters and ghetto heroes.

But the films became popular especially among Black Americans, and Vonetta came back home to Hollywood to become a star in one of the genre's most famous movies - the Black horror film "Blacula" with co-star William Marshall. She went on to display her beauty in many other films, especially as star of the sexy "Melinda" in which her beauty was amply displayed.

A highlight of her career was co-starring with Clint Eastwood as his first and only Black love interest in "The Eiger Sanction", but it was also Eastwood's only box office flop

My favourite film of hers was "Thomasine and Bushrod" which she made with her then partner Max Julien, the handsome writer, producer and star of "The Mack" -- the famous Black gangster-pimp movie that busted the box office and made him rich and famous. The financial and box-office success of "The Mack" gave Vonetta and Max the chance to collaborate in their own very sassy Black Western version of the Bonnie and Clyde story, "Thomasine & Bushrod".

It was a beautiful movie, even if it wasn't as big a hit as they hoped, but it was good enough that even today it is still shown on late night TV.

I had been surprised but delighted when Vonetta invited me to come and visit her in Los Angeles while they were editng the film. I had been back home in Jamaica for just two years but nothing was happening and I had never seen California, so of course I accepted. I was in the studio when they edited the *'Thomasine & Bushrod"* soundtrack and they used my voice to dub a little section of the story, so I'm proud to say I have had a role in a Hollywood movie!

Vonetta and Max were the biggest stars in the Black Hollywood firmament. Like Beyonce and JayZ today, they were the Black Hollywood 'It" couple -- each famous in their own right and famous as a couple. Staying with them was a true introduction to Hollywood. They moved in the right circles with all the famous entertainment stars of film and music, Black and White, as well as the White producers and directors who ran the business side of the industry.

Being in their company was being in the VIP star lane of Red Carpet flashbulbs and autographs. It was a very nice thing to happen to a good friend and I got to enjoy it when she shared it with me.

Vonetta and Max lived in an apartment one block from the famous Hollywood Boulevard, but they had just bought and were restoring a fabulous property in the exclusive Coldwater Canyon hills overlooking Los Angeles. They had bought the house from a famous rock artist whose name I am not allowed to mention because of the many drug-taking syringes that had to be cleaned out of the house first.

The building was all made of pine wood – walls, floors, ceiling, shelves, cupboards, floors. It was unique and beautiful, with a high 360-degree view over the city and surrounding hills.

Vonetta got me helping her clean it from top to bottom. First we had to wipe all the wood with pine oil, rather like painting walls except with pine oil. It took a while, one room at a time over several days but we enjoyed the work, sustaining ourselves with a buffet of delicious meals, cold snacks and juices we brought up with us each day from the gourmet restaurants at the foot of the hill.

The house had four bedrooms and mine had its own verandah overlooking the mountains. Further along the driveway, the property also had a two- bedroom guest house. We spent a lot of time going up and down the hill as we fixed up the house, bought and brought up materials and furnishings.

I was glad to be Vonetta's girlfriend helping her fix up her house. She smiled indulgently to see and hear me talk about becoming a Rasta, wearing skirts instead of the trousers I always used to wear to cover my skinny legs, and covering my hair in typical Rastawoman styles. Rasta was something new to Vonetta, but she had been part of the 'Black is Beautiful' movement in California and both Angela Davis and Huey Newton – founder of the Black Panthers – were personal friends. To her, Rasta was Jamaica's version of the same revolution, and she was proud to have a friend who could share information about what was happening in Jamaica.

Max had written another film, the action heroine drama *"Cleopatra Jones"* and the studio was once again allowing him to direct, so he was busy with all the pre-production details and we hardly saw him in the days. He had written the lead role for Vonetta and she was looking forward to starring in another movie.

We also gave ourselves time off to enjoy Los Angeles – the restaurants, shops and the nightclubs. Staying with Vonetta gave me an insider's look at Hollywood and the film industry, the people who work in it, the city of Los Angeles and its studios, its leisure spots, it's star quality. We would often stop by night clubs, attend cocktail parties thrown by studio executives, have drinks at special celebrity bars, or end the night at a pavement burger joint that was world famous for its special sauce.

Hollywood was just as it is in the movies. Especially if you are in the movies.

Vonetta was a big movie star, so I met a lot of other movie stars in Vonetta's company.

For instance, Vonetta and Max's lawyer was also Groucho Marx's lawyer and while waiting in the lobby for Max to finish a meeting, I was introduced to the famous comedian. It was amazing to have this very famous man smile and sit down beside me to say Hello. He was old, but he still had a twinkle in his eye for a pretty woman!

There was always a party, a premiere, a dinner, a friend's house to go to, another celebrity to meet. They were everywhere.

In Vonetta's company I met all the stars of the Blacksploitation movies. Pam Grier, Ken Norton, Jim Brown,

Fred Williamson, William Marshall, Paula Kelly, Rosalind Cash, Gloria Hendry.

In Vonetta's company I also met all the Black stars of popular music. Stevie Wonder, Quincy Jones, Billy Paul, Dionne Warrick, Diana Ross, Minnie Ripperton at parties, at premieres, at night clubs. Even in the supermarket, where I bumped into Ernest Borgnine – remember him?

It was fun. I loved it.

At the Cannes Film Festival two years earlier, I had been sitting a few feet away from Robert Redford sitting on the verandah of the Carlton Hotel bar watching the people walking on the Croisette avenue below. He was certainly the biggest star I had ever seen close up. I didn't ask for his autograph, just smiled, because I was impressed but not too much. He smiled back and I could see he was glad I hadn't bothered him more than that. Always the best way with celebrities.

Vonetta was always pleased to introduce her girlfriend from Jamaica.

Jamaica!

You're from Jamaica!

Say something, let me hear you speak!

Sing some reggae!

I LOVE Jamaica!

Are you in movies too!

To them, I was special because I was Jamaican. In their eyes Jamaica was a magical place. To them, Jamaica was '*Doctor No*' and Montego Bay and Rum Punch drinks on white sand beaches.

Who was I to tell them different?

Beautiful Jamaica! Yeah mon!

So one morning, as I was sewing red, gold and green sequins onto the lapels of a black jacket to wear to a premiere Vonetta was taking me to, I had the idea that it would be a good move to bring some of the Black Hollywood films to Jamaica and show them in a 'film festival' just like the Cannes Film Festival. There wasn't a film festival anywhere for Black films, so why didn't I make one in Jamaica?

I asked Vonetta what she thought of the idea and she was excited. She thought it was the best thing that could happen to the Black film industry that had become Hollywood's most popular genre. She felt that it would be good for Black Hollywood to have a special event to honour their works, and having it in Jamaica would be the most perfect location. All we had to do was get the films and show them in Jamaica.

How?

Vonetta just laughed, "I can get them all for you."

She picked up the phone and called someone and said "Hi! How would you like to show your film at a festival in Jamaica?" She squealed with excitement, then laughed. "I'm coming to lunch and bringing my Jamaican friend Barbara with me."

The name 'Jamaica' was gold. Jamaica was considered an even more desirable destination than Hollywood or Los Angeles, believe me. There is no one in the world who doesn't want to come to Jamaica. And this was before Bob Marley made Jamaica even more desirable.

The independent film distribution companies were glad to become involved ,because of the tight grip that the sole film distributor in Jamaica had been exercising on the films selected for screening in Jamaica. In typically raciall prejudiced practice, he had been excluding all the Black films, so this was a good opportunity for them to get exposure and the studios were very pleased. One by one, with Vonetta's contacts, we lined up seven major feature films and a documentary on a big Black music show.

With films promised, we made a list of stars who should be invited who would make the event news. Vonetta got out her phone book and called up all her movie star friends and asked them if they were interested. Of course they were!

Jim Brown, Rosalind Cash, Paula Kelly, William Marshall ... the list started getting long. Optimistically, we hoped the studios would pay expenses to fly their stars to Jamaica, but none agreed to this arrangement. We would have to find an airline in need of publicity.

Now it was time to see if I could sell the idea to Jamaica. Having once been the Public Relations person in London for the Jamaica Tourist Board, I knew that there was funding available to help make this event happen if approval was granted from the top.

So I decided to go to the real top, to my girlfriend Beverley Manley, the Prime Minister's wife. She and I had been extras in the film "*A High Wind in Jamaica*' that had been filmed in Jamaica and that had brought us both to London to continue filming indoor scenes. We had decided to stay on in England, where she and I had shared a London flat.

Beverley was now the wife of the Prime Minister and First Lady of Jamaica. Since returning home, Beverley had worked with Perry Henzell's film production company and she even had a role in "*The Harder They Come*". I told Vonetta I was sure Beverley could get the Prime Minister to support our plan.

"Call her," she said, handing me the phone.

I found Beverley's number in my phone book and called her.

"Would you and Michael agree to be Patron of the first Jamaica Film Festival? I can bring some of the top Black Hollywood films and film stars to Jamaica for it."

Beverley was so excited. "Definitely, Barbara. Great idea! I'll speak to Michael right away and get his approval. Then I will get the Tourist Board to take charge this end."

And so said, so done.

Within days – and a few lunches with film executives at nice restaurants around Hollywood – Vonetta had arranged for seven films to be entered in the first Jamaica Film Festival. She got agreements from the heads of studios, which is a higher level than the producers of the films, for their films to be shown in Jamaica. This high level approval was soon to prove invaluable.

Meanwhile Beverley called to say that 'the Prime

Minister and his wife' would be Patrons of the Jamaica Film Festival (some media began calling it the Jamaica BLACK Film Festival) and that the Jamaica Tourist Board would make all arrangements for guest accommodation.

My father, the well-known journalist Evon Blake, proud that the Prime Minister and Tourist Board were supporting his daughter, called up an old friend who happened to be the CEO of Eastern Airlines, and told him to get involved. Thanks to that call, Eastern agreed to fly a planeload of stars from Los Angeles, via Atlanta to Kingston and back just for the free publicity.

Just like that, we had a film festival. We opened a bottle of chilled, dry white wine to celebrate.

With our plans bubbling, I enjoyed the rest of my stay in Los Angeles happily following in Vonetta's star spangled footsteps.

I got to meet boxer Ken Norton, fit and fabulous at the height of his career before the fight with Ali that everyone said he won, and enjoying the fame of his short career as a very handsome movie star in the racially controversial film "*Mandingo*". Invited with Vonetta to lunch with him, we met at his gym just as he was about to do some exercise in the ring.

"Keep these for me," he said, peeling the many gold and jeweled ornaments from his fingers, wrists and neck into my hands. Shocked, I bundled the heavy handful of rubies, sapphires and diamonds into my handbag, making sure to hand them back carefully when he finished and we were leaving the gym.

"He's trying to impress you," Vonetta smiled.

"I know. He's cute, but he's married," I said.

*

I got to meet Stevie Wonder in a VIP box upstairs a Hollywood Boulevard night club.

"Stevie, meet my friend Barbara from Jamaica."

Stevie smiled and stretched out his hand.

My "Hi" was inaudible over the club's music.

I smiled. We shook hands.

I knew he couldn't see me.

Two days later Stevie sent two first class air tickets for Vonetta and her Jamaican friend to attend his show in San Francisco. Vonetta is from San Francisco and loved the opportunity to visit her mother at their home there. We flew over to San Francisco and went to the star dressing room backstage.

"Stevie, remember my friend Barbara from Jamaica?"

Stevie smiled and reaches out a hand again.

I didn't know what to say, but I smiled again.

Minnie Ripperton came in, hugged Stevie and my moment was over.

It wasn't till years later, when he came to Jamaica for a show, that I got to speak to him again at a crowded cocktail party and say "Hi, I am Vonetta's friend. We met in L.A. and you sent us tickets to your show. Welcome to my home."

He gave a big smile of recognition and talked to me happily for a while, holding tight to my hand and arm, asking me which month I am born in and when I said June, calling me "My Jamaican Gemini."

*

This desribes a typical Hollywood evening:

A film director and his wife invite us for dinner at a fancy restaurant, with drinks first at their Bel Air home. Bel Air looks just like in the movies. Tall palm trees line the sidewalks and expensive homes line the avenues. Even more stunning than the expensive homes sitting way back from the pavement on smoothly manicured lawns, are the expensive cars parked in the long driveways – Bentleys, Rolls Royces, Jaguars, Porsches, Lamborghinis. There is a look of MONEY everywhere.

The mansion we are visiting stretches wide and low from the outside and is vast inside. A uniformed maid opens the huge double doors and shows us the way forward. The lights are low in the vast living room of the house. We pass through the vast dining room with 12-seater dining table, then pass the soft cushions and sofa-chairs of the cinema lounge, through the pool table room, the library and finally emerge in a section on the other side of the swimming pool, where we drink really good dry white wine and look over the lights of Los Angeles.

The lady of the house picks up a phone and speaks into it.

A chef in apron and cap appears.

"Would you like some shrimp on toast with your wine?" the lady of the house asks us.

Of course we would.

The chef comes back with a large plate covered with fat shrimp sizzling on garlic bread, a chili cream dip and a huge, beautiful salad of lettuce, avocado slices, palm tree hearts, asparagus, red cabbage and little cherry tomatoes.

This is a meal itself, better than any restaurant.

The chef returns with a sizzling platter.

"The grill was hot, so the chef put on some lamb chops." the lady of the house smiles.

Boiled corns on skewers.

Baked potatoes with whipped butter.

The lady of the house brings out the spliffs.

We forget about going to a restaurant.

*

This describes a Hollywood day:

Vonetta is shopping for fabrics in a store displaying some of the most beautiful fabrics I've ever seen.

Satins, silks, tafettas, laces. All so beautiful.

She's going to teach me how to cut and sew something from a pattern.

Yes, Vonetta can use a sewing machine to make clothes. She is proud of that skill.

Across on another aisle is Diana Ross examing the fabrics.

"Hi, Miss Ross," Vonetta calls sweetly.

Diana Ross looks up from behind plate-sized dark glasses, sees Vonetta and waves her fingers gently.

Can I go over and ask for an autograph?

"Don't you dare, Barbara. It's not done."

I smile at Diana Ross.

She doesn't register my eye contact.

Vonetta buys me some red taffeta fabric with green, gold and black stripes, and a pattern for a short, long-sleeved jacket. She buys herself some fabric and a pattern too.

We go back to the apartment and set up the sewing machine.

(I still have the jacket she taught me to make.)

*

This describes an evening with Vonetta and Max:

Billy Paul comes over to the apartment for dinner. His song *"Me and Mrs. Jones"* is Number One on the Hit Parade. He and Max are good friends.

I cook chicken Jamaican style with lots of gravy, mashed potatoes and spinach. They say how great my chicken tastes.

Billy says he must look for a Jamaican woman to cook chicken for him.

We laugh, and I say "Come to Jamaica, man."

Billy and Max spend the night laughing and talking and listening to music and talking about music. They argue and disagree about which song they like best.

They drink red wine and smoke pot.

They enjoy each other's company.

Vonetta is happy to see her man happy.

The studio has just told Max that Vonetta can't play the role of *"Cleopatra Jones"* in the film that he wrote for her.

It's going to another actress. Tamara Dobson.

They are both unhappy about that, but they have to accept it.

The studio is the boss. What the studio says, goes.

That's a shame.

Big disappointment.

Still, Max gets to direct it.

The money he is earning pays for the pine wood mansion. The pine wood mansion is ready for Max and Vonetta to move in.

It smells so nice. Like living in a pine tree.

I finish sewing the red, gold and green sequins on my black jacket. I plan to wear it on opening night of the Jamaica Film Festival.

Hollywood, is just like in the movies!

THE JAMAICA FILM FESTIVAL

The Jamaica Tourist Board bosses were very annoyed to find they had to support my BLACK film festival. They all were staunch supporters of the previous JLP administration, and had no love for Michael and Beverly, their PNP Prime Minister and First Lady.

Worst of all, to have to support something BLACK was anathema to them. When I used to work in London for their PR company, the Tourist Board only promoted White people in their PR and pictures aimed exclusively at White people. In those days Black people were only servants in tourism promotion, never the topic of a special JTB event. So they were really upset.

But when my father used his good friend, the head of Eastern Airlines, to get him to fly the movie stars free from Los Angeles to Jamaica, they were impressed. Eastern was a major airline in those days. The Tourist Board arranged for the Sheraton Kingston Hotel to house the stars, and I booked the Carib Cinema to show the films, one each night at 8:30.

The Palace Amusement Company that held the monopoly on showing Hollywood films, had the same attitude to me as the Tourist Board. Black films were NOT on their schedule and the cinema owners were the kind of 'imitation White' Jamaicans who hated any and everything Black.

They tried several excuses to stop the film festival happening, but the studio bosses in Hollywood were so glad of the opportunity to break into what seemed a closed market, they insisted that Palace should allow it to happen or they would block them with their Hollywood community, which was almost all White (and Jewish) from getting any more of their usual films. With the Prime Minister and the Tourist Board in charge, they had to fit in.

I flew up to Atlanta to meet the plane full of Black Hollywood stars, directors and some journalists. We all travelled on that historic Eastern Airlines flight from Hollywood to Jamaica, via Atlanta, where we had breakfast at a grand hotel hosted by Ambassador Andrew Young and Atlanta Mayor Maynard Jackson. I realized how important those two Black men were, when the Black Hollywood stars who I was in awe of, were in awe of them. They were so shy about being around those two men.

As organizer of the event, I got to sit at their table, where they made polite conversation with Jim Brown, the only one of the stars who was at ease with them. Jim Brown, of course, had already been a big star as a football hero, and film was just his next step on the ladder. He was very cool, a really nice man. He had been given two tickets for the flight, but didn't bring a guest with him.

As the seat next to his was the only vacant seat on the flight to Jamaica, I sat beside him.

Andrew Young – then Mayor of Atlanta – hosted the planeload of stars at breakfast while we waited for the Jamaica flight. As well as Jim Brown – at the time the biggest Black film hearthrob, there was Rosalind Cash who co-starred with Charlton Heston in of *'Planet of the Apes"*; dancer-actress Paula Kelly - co-star with Shirley McLaine in *"Sweet Charity"*; William Marshall, star of *'Blacula'*; Gloria Hendry, first Black Bond Girl with Roger Moore in *"Live & Let Die"*; Bernie Casey, former basketballer and star of *"Maurie* – one of the festival films; Ivan Dixon, star of *"The Spook That Sat By The Door"* and the film's director and book author, Sam Greenlee; and two documentary film makers Stan Lathan and Matt Robinson with their music doc *"Save The Children"* that won many awards and led to their prosperous careers in film and television.

My only disappointment was that Vonetta and Max didn't come. She had accepted a role as Clint Eastwood's first Black co-star in the film *"The Eiger Sanction"*. For her, this was the breakthrough of a lifetime, starring in a major Hollywood movie with a major White star.

Max was furious that she had turned down a chance to show their film at a major Black Hollywood event she had helped organize in beautiful Jamaica. It was the start of the end of their relationship, sorry to say. Plus, the Eastwood film turned out to be a major box office flop. I was sad, remembering how the Jamaica Film Festival was born and who was its chief godmother, but I put my mind to all I had to do to make the event happen to make her proud of having helped.

We landed in Montego Bay to flashbulbs, a welcome calypso band, the Mayor of Montego Bay and the Director of Tourism. Vonetta would have loved the drama of it!

On our arrival, you could see from the look on the Tourism Director Anthony Abrahams' face when he saw Jim Brown, Rosalind Cash and Paula Kelly, how surprised everyone was that I had actually pulled it off and brought all these Black movie stars to Jamaica.

After a preview party that night at one of the many fabulous mansions on the Ironshore Estate overlooking Montego Bay, the stars were flown to another grand welcome in Kingston. Seeing the help the Black American head of Eastern Airlines gave to fly 38 people from Hollywood to Jamaica, the Tourist Board fell behind us meekly. They arranged free accommodation at the Sheraton Kingston hotel and the hotel became the centre of the film festival.

Everyone was so excited to meet real movie stars, and Black ones at that. The Sheraton Hotel was a beautiful meeting place and the film festival took over the building and especially the poolside, where the bar was kept busy with people coming and going to meet the stars.

We showed one feature film each night of six nights, then held an Awards Ceremony on the last night at the Sheraton Ballroom. The films were: *'Save The Children'* a music documentary by Stan Lathan, who went on to make many brilliant TV series and shows; *'Uptown Saturday Night"* a comedy starring Bill Cosby Harry and Belafonte;

'*Maurie*' with Bernie Casey, who was one of the stars who came to Jamaica.

We also showed "*The Autobiography of Miss Jane Pittman*" starring Cicely Tyson, who did not come but who was awarded the Best Actress award; '*Thomasine and Bushrod*", starring Vonetta McGee and Max Julien.We were also supposed to show "*The Spook That Sat By The Door*", the film of the book by Sam Greenlee, but Palace Amusement Company said the film 'did not arrive in Jamaica'. Sam was furious. We didn't know then that it was a lie.

I still have some photos and newspaper clippings of Prime Minister Michael Manley at his most handsome and cool, entertaining some of the Black stars at a party at the official residence of Mayor of Kingston Ralph Brown, the City's host.

My favourite photo is of beautiful Beverly, wife of the Prime Minister, my great girlfriend and the other guardian angel who with Vonetta made the film festival happen, at the cinema on Opening Night. She wears her signature Afro as she sits beside her best friends – Antiguan socialite Solange Barakat and white Jamaican heiress Angela Desnoes of the Desnoes & Geddes Red Strips beer company, wearing a Rasta tam.

Behind them in the picture is Neville Garrick, who later made all the Bob Marley album covers and stage backdrops. I had met him when he was Art Director of the Jamaica Daily News newspaper we both were working on, and I invited him to design a logo for our letterhead, as we could not afford to advertise.

Neville came with me when I went to ask Bob Marley if the Wailers would play at the Film Festival Awards event. Bob said yes, but we couldn't afford the Wailers fee so they never played at our event. However, as a result of that meeting, Neville went on to become the artist for Bob Marley's albums and stage backdrops, traveling the world with him.

Beside Neville sat 'the Black Bond girl' Gloria Hendry, next to her William Marshall, star of the Black horror film *'Blacula'*. Gloria made a big fuss one evening saying 'all her jewelry' had been stolen, but she quieted down when the other stars on the trip said she was lying and hadn't brought any jewelry with her.

At the end of the film festival, when the Awards show was over and I was going home, my father gave me Sixty Dollars which he said was all the money that had been made selling tickets. We made no money whatsoever.

My father was disgusted with me, but it was his fault. He had trusted our tickets and business to a man who had persuaded my father he was a much better person to handle the business than my bearded, truck-driving, Rastaman whom I lived with, and convinced my father he would take good care of the tickets. I didn't trust him, but my father had given him the keys to the room in which we had stored the tickets.

With that freedom, he had duplicated the tickets, sold the fake tickets himself and made all the money. (He built a house at Harbour View later with his newfound prosperity, but it was overcome by the sea in a hurricane years later. Karma.)

My father hardly spoke to me after that, saying the film festival had been a flop. I hope it was because he was ashamed of the decision he made on the tickets that had deprived us of our well-earned benefits, but it was a sad moment after all that hard work. My father and I returned to our previous relationship in which we loved each other, but hardly spoke, and we grew further apart as I embraced Rastafari ever more fully. (It wasn't till many years later when I gave birth to his grandson Makonnen that our relationship became close again.)

I had planned that Bob Marley and the Wailers would play at the Awards, but in the end we could not afford them. Tony Laing, the great show producer, directed the Film Festival Awards show with Fab Five as the band and Neville Willoughby, the leading radio announcer and talk-show host, handling the announcements. Patsy Yuen, a beautiful Chinese girl who was Miss Jamaica, handed out the trophies - carved wooden maps of Jamaica with Parishes each inlaid with different colourful woods.

Douglas Morrow, the white producer of the film *"Maurie"* that was one of the films I showed, gave me an Award of a United Nations Peace Medal, a large silver coin with engraved writing on either side and the UN logo, in a velvet presentation case.

He was the only white person in the group of actors

and film directors who came from Los Angeles and was the only person who brought me a gift. It was the first award I ever received.

So the first Jamaica Film Festival finally came to a close. I remember that after the show I could have disappeared into the Kingston night with Jim Brown. It was a very serious invitation and choice.

But I didn't want that kind of Hollywood ending.

Instead I went home to bed by myself and slept for 24 hours.

* * *

Looking back, I realize even more now what a great achievement the first Film Festival was. In fact, the second Jamaica Film Festival ended with the patrons rioting and mashing up the cinema, all because Jamaicans wanted to see a movie.

Sam Greenlee was not happy to learn that his film *"The Spook That Sat By The Door"* had not arrived in Jamaica for the first film festival. The film was a story of a Black former CIA agent who leaves the service and instead uses what he has learned in counter-intelligence to train a group of Black ghetto youths to become revolutionaries.

It was a very Black conscious film in the era of Black Power and in a world where Angela Davis, George Jackson and Malcolm X were current heroes and role models. The film had become famous in the global Black revolutionary movement and Jamaicans had heard about it and hoped to see it at the first Jamaica Film Festival.

However, the cinema owners Palace Amusement Company, to whom all the films had been shipped, said that "Spook" had not arrived in Jamaica, and Sam spent the entire film festival complaining and trying to find out what had happened to his film. When he checked with his people back in the USA, they confirmed the film had been shipped, and records showed it had arrived in Jamaica. But Palace Amusement Company, which handled everything to do with films coming into Jamaica, said they had not received it.

So Sam decided to come to the second Jamaica Film Festival and bring his own copy of the film with him so he could have the pleasure of seeing it with a Black Jamaican audience.

We moved the second festival to the State Theatre, whose proprietor Dudley McMillan had been suffering financially from a lack of any independent films to show except Japanese karate movies, and therefore hoped to get a link to the independent Black films my festival had shown.

We didn't have many films this second year, but Vonetta came to Jamaica that year to make up for missing the first festival, and we showed *"Thomasine & Bushrod"* again. We showed the feature *"One People"*, the first film from Surinam and our programme included a long and boring film from China, but there was a packed cinema the night *"The Spook"* was to be shown.

I was waiting for the lights to dim when my man sent a friend to my seat who told me I was to be taken home as there was going to be trouble. Minutes after I left, a Police officer came on stage and announced that according to the new law that had just been passed to curb crime in Jamaica, it was illegal to show guns in films, so *"The Spook"* could not be shown.

The audience rioted. They tore the place apart, seats, carpets, everything. The cinema was completely destroyed. The next morning's light showed a burnt-out hollow space, with wrecked chairs and blackened walls. No films were ever shown there again, and the owner turned it into an art gallery. I have no idea who did it and no one was ever arrested and charged with the crime.

Years later the world learned that the US government intelligence agencies were directly involved in suppressing *"The Spook That Sat By The Door"* and ensuring that it was blocked from screening everywhere, as they considered it a dangerous incentive for Black revolution. It was a major blow to the profits of the film and also to Sam Greenlee's literary career and fortunes. Jamaica had been just one stop in a global blockade.

You can see the film for free today on YouTube, but Sam Greenlee is no longer in this world.

* * *

When I began organizing the third Jamaica Film Festival a year later, I was working in the Office of the Prime Minister. Out of work and with no income, I had asked Prime

Minister Michael Manley for a job. He placed me in his Jamaica House office as Assistant to Senator Arnold Bertram, the Minister of Culture, who was one of the leading Marxists directing the political actions of the PNP Government.

I had hoped the job he gave me would be something to do with television or film,, so I was disappointed to find that the job was little more than answering the phone and typing letters like a secretary for the Minister, while more important political matters were discussed daily in his tightly closed office with the PNP's leading Marxist-Leninists who came to the office to communicate with their political advisors in Cuba.

As I began planning the next film festival, Bertram sent me on assignment to the Tourist Board office Montego Bay, far away from the centre of activity and handed the film festival organizing over to Jessica Jones, a White Jamaican employee of the Tourist Board. It was hard to swallow seeing my idea taken over by those who could never duplicate my effort or do better, but I had no other choice but to watch in silence.

When the event opened at the Carib Cinema, I came over to Kingston for one night to sit with my Cuban film maker friend Segio Giral, whose invitation to Jamaica I had promised when we first met in Cuba two years before. He was surprised not to see me on stage running the show. I was embarrassed at how small the audience was, how un-special the 'film festival' was and how obvious it was that those who knew nothing about film had presented such a poor show.

After that, I stopped trying to organize another Jamaica Film Festival.

Only the Reggae Film Festivals I organized 40 years later came close to the impact and popularity of the first Jamaica Film Festival.

Others have tried, but failed. In 2015 a Government employee of the office that registers copyright spent a budget of 8 Million Dollars organizing a 'Jamaica Film Festival', despite my protest at her using the name of my event. She said since I hadn't copyrighted the name, she was free to use it, and hired the leading and most expensive lawyers to write me challenging my claim. I could not afford to do anything about it, so I sat back and waited on JAH.

JAH was not sleeping. Her effort was a major disaster, heavily criticized and never repeated. The embarassment was so great she immediately left Jamaica to live in one of the small Caribbean islands.

The first Jamaica Film Festival was a once-in-a-lifetime experience and an achievement that I am very, very proud of. I didn't make any money, but it didn't cost me a penny to do it and it was a great experience and achievement.

Thank you so much Vonetta McGee.

Thank you so much Beverly Manley

CUBA, LEIPZIG AND IRAQ

One of the most interesting trips of my life was to Iraq in 1977 as a guest of a Festival of Palestinian Films. It was also the scene of what I used to consider one of my most stupid acts, but let me explain everything first.

A great blessing that resulted from the second Jamaica Film Festival was that a few months later the Cuban Embassy asked me to organize a Cuban Film Week in Kingston for the famous Cuban Film Institute, ICAIC. The Ambassador introduced me to the Cuban Cultural Attache, Jesus Cos Cause, a young Black man who was a highly-respected poet in his country.

Cos Cause was in his early 20s and a devoted revolutionary. At our first meeting he told me in Spanish that he would not be speaking English with me, as that was the language of the 'American occupiers' who Fidel's revolution had overthrown. Spanish had been one of my best subjects at Wolmers Girls School, thanks to our teacher Miss Ferez who was Latino. My grammar and vocabulary were good, but I had no practice and was shy to speak it to this Cuban.

However, he put a dictionary before me and said I should use it to look up any Spanish words I needed. With that instruction, I dug deep into my Spanish classes and overcame my shyness. It served me well and thanks to Jesus

Cos Cause, I can now call myself completely bi-lingual in Spanish. I can even take shorthand in Spanish now! Thank you Cuban Film Institute.

We arranged a week-long screening of five of Cuba's best films. Cuba believed that film should serve the Revolution, whether feature or documentary, and their films were an interesting collection of a new type of storytelling. Cuban films were just being seen outside the country, and the world was raving about them.

Two that stand out were *"La Ultima Cena"* (*"The Last Supper"*) about a slave plantation whose absentee owner arrives with the magnanimous plan to celebrate Holy Week by having dinner with twelve selected slaves and then giving all the slaves a holiday on Good Friday. The plantation overseer is opposed to this plan, saying nothing good will come of it.

The slaves are uncomfortable sitting in their rags at the owner's grand dinner table, but they endure and enjoy the experience. One by one as the dinner unfolds they tell him their stories of who and what they were before being taken and enslaved.

One of the slaves at the table is a perpetual runaway, who has been so brutalized each time he is recaptured, that he is missing an ear and his body shows signs of torture. When his turn to speak comes, he says that next time he escapes he will not be caught because he will transform himself into the wind, a river, a tree.

On Good Friday the slaves start enjoying the promised

holiday, but the overseer refuses to acknowledge the day off and starts beating them to return to work. The slaves riot and this spooks the horses drawing a carriage in which the plantation owner's daughter is riding. The carriage crashes off a cliff and the daughter dies, so the plantation owner regrets his decision and orders even more brutality as revenge.

Each of the twelve slaves who sat at his dinner table are hunted down and killed, their heads impaled on high poles around the site of a proposed chapel.

It's the usual story of the slave-master winning through brutality. But as the film ends, you see that there are only eleven heads impaled, with one pole still empty. Then the scene changes and we see a river rushing by, a tall tree standing strong, and an eagle flying high in the sky. "*La Ultima Cena*" is still one of Cuba's most famous films.

Another film was "*The Schoolteacher'*, based on the time when Fidel closed the universities and told the students to go out and teach the illiterate population to read and write. It was an action that started Cuba's 100% literacy rate and the film told a good story to illustrate it.

A young student arrives in a rural village, where the older peasants laugh at the prospect of this 'child' teaching them anything, so they hardly attend his classes.

The schoolteacher spends his days exploring the countryside and one day he comes across a spot where he can see that preparations are being made to welcome a 'Bay of Pigs' invasion. He alerts the community and the invasion is thwarted. The teacher becomes a hero and the peasants fill his classroom.

These were the kind of films Cuba was making and the event was well attended each night. Two film makers came to Jamaica with the films. One was a journalist Marisol, who worked as a writer with the Cuban Film Institute ICAIC, where not only were films made but film magazines published and the beautiful Cuban film posters produced that became collectors' items around the world.

As thanks, when the film festival was over the Cuban Embassy invited me to visit Cuba as a guest of the famous Cuban Film Institute ICAIC.

I arrived in Havana, where Marisol met me and spent a week showing me her country. She took me to the ICAIC headquarters where I spent two days viewing films that I had wished to see but were unavailable in the West, such as D.W. Griffiths' film *"Birth Of A Nation"* - a film that had promoted, strengthened and justified the Klu Klux Klan and was banned for screening in the USA because of how it incited and justified racial violence, especially lynching.

I got to see footage of performances ofthe great singer, actor and intellectual Paul Robeson, who was blacklisted by the USA for finding a greater welcome for his talent and intellect in Socialist Russia than America. There were the historic films of Oscar Micheaux, the first Black film maker in the 1930s who made great feature films starring Black actors that were shown to Black audiences. I had never heard of him before Cuba.

At ICAIC I met Santiago Alvarez, the great documentary film maker who was the dean and chief inspiration of Cuban films and film makers. We became great friends, as he showed me around the historic parts of Havana and talked of the history of the Revolution. "Film must serve the public, not the pockets of film makers. Film is too valuable to waste," he lectured. "There must be a lesson to teach a new way forward, or we are just making cotton candy for children."

Marisol flew me to Santiago on the other side of the island, then we drove along a highway lined with piles of stones each bearing the name of a fallen fighter. Telling me the history of the revolution that she had experienced, I cannot forget one thing she said about it with tears in her eyes:

"Demasiado sangre! Demasiado sangre!" she wept. "Too much blood! Too much blood!!!"

I saw that the price of the Revolution had been costly, not just for those who died, but especially for those still alive.

At a grand reception in Havana one night shortly before leaving Cuba, I was introduced to a grand blonde lady who I was told was the director of the Leipzig Film Festival in East Germany. With a smile she invited me to be a member of the Jury for the 21st Festival taking place later that year.

I had no idea where Leipzig was, but I accepted with pleasure.

LEIPZIG - BEHIND THE IRON CURTAIN

1976

I discovered Leipzig was 'behind the Iron Curtain" the section of Europe containing all the countries controlled by Russia. I was apprehensive. What had I let myself in for? But new adventures were always welcome.

I flew from Kingston to New York, London and West Berlin, Germany, then by separate plane to Leipzig. As the plane took off from West Berlin heading over the border into East Germany, the lights of cities and homes below disappeared and there was just an inky darkness. It seemed ominous. I knew I was in a world unprotected by Western laws and governments. I was behind the Iron Curtain.

The XXI Leipzig International film Festival took place when Germany was still divided into East and West, and the East was a Communist state supported by Russia. The festival's motto was '*Films of the World for the Peace of the World*" and it was attended by film makers and activists from the world's most controversial places where there was war between West and East, Capitalism versus Socialism and Communism.

We landed in East Germany and there seemed to be soldiers everywhere. The streets were lit, but the buildings were all in darkness. I was beginning to be very worried as a car drove me to the Film Festival headquarters, but once there things changed completely.

A smiling lady offered me a small glass of vodka in which three coffee beans were flaming a blue light and giving off a smell that reminded me of Jamaica. I had never seen a drink like that and I realised this would be an experience like no other. I blew out the flames, sipped my drink and relaxed. It was going to be OK.

First I needed a warm coat, so I was taken to a government clothing shop where I picked a big brown fake fur coat that was so beautiful, that years later my movie star girlfriend Vonetta borrowed it to wear to a film script audition!

Then I was taken on tour of the town centre where stalls had been set up to sell Christmas things – toys, craft, brightly-wrapped presents, bright red Poinsettia potted plants, delicious cakes and piles of raisins, currants, cherries, cinnamon, cloves and seasonings for making cakes. I could see that there was a lot in Leipzig to bring Christmas cheer.

Being a member of the film festival Jury was a prestigious role and I was given very special treatment every day, everywhere. It was wonderful to meet again Santiago Alvarez, the great Cuban film maker, and to be able to join his conversations with the other film makers.

I was wearing my hair in an Afro that made people associate me with Angela Davis and I am told that some in the audience thought I was her when I was introduced on stage. I hardly remember the other jurors, but I remember the film makers and their films. The films were all about revolutions taking place, especially in Africa.

I met several very young African students who were refugees from the South African anti-apartheid struggle in Soweto and some Cuban film makers who had been in Angola as soldiers. The Cubans brought film of their activities in various African countries where Cuba was helping fight wars of liberation from European colonial masters.

I made friends with a lot of people, especially Vu Nam, an old documentary film maker from Viet Nam who refused to speak French because it was an 'occupation language', so all our conversations had to be translated from Vietnamese to French, then to English so I could understand him. People had strong political beliefs. Vu Nam had never met a Black woman before, and he 'adopted' me as his 'daughter', drawing a lovely portrait of me that was all Afro and big eyes.

Seeing such an amazing collection of people and experiences, I said out loud that I wished I had a film camera to record it. No sooner had I said that, than I was offered a film crew of a cameraman and sound technician from GDR-TV to make a documentary on the festival. With joy I turned on my TV journalist role and filmed interviews and footage of the Festival.

When the ceremony was finished in Leipzig, I was given a hotel room in East Berlin and a room in GDR-TV offices to edit my footage into my very first, very own documentary film edited in the process of that time where we ran separate rolls of 16mm film and sound rolls, cutting them separately but together. I called my film *'The Peaceful Gun – Films of the World for the Peace of the World."*

It was quite an experience to be 'behind the Iron Curtain' in East Germany, first at Leipzig and then when the Festival was over, in East Berlin. While we stayed there waiting for our flight, I got an offer to do what other East Germans could not, which was cross over the famous Wall into West Germany at the Brandenberg Gate. The offer was made by two Spanish-speaking women who came into our hotel lobby and started speaking to me and the Cubans who were relaxing with us.

They were as gracious as tour guides, but I wasn't stupid enough to betray my hosts and my own beliefs to come with them for a look at the other side of the Wall. I knew that anyone who wanted to escape Cuba could receive 'asylum' in the West by crossing the border wall into West Germany. I didn't need to escape, but even just going on a sightseeing tour would be seen as a betrayal of the principles of my Cuban friends and especially my East German hosts.

Thanks to East Germany, I was now a real film maker with a film of my own. I carried it back home in two film cans, one with the film strip and one with the sound tape, hoping to 'marry' them together (that was the process for 16mm film making in those days). But I couldn't get permisson from the Governent to use the Jamaica Information Service to do that, and eventually in frustration I agreed to send the cans to a film maker friend in New York who promised to do the 'marrying'. I never heard from him again and never saw my film again.

A film maker I made friends with in Leipzig was a ginger-haired Israeli Jew who, surprisingly, had made a film supporting the Palestinian cause. I, good little revolutionary that I was, spent quite a lot of time talking with him and learning more about the Palestinians struggle for their land and their rights.

As a result of those conversations, when I got back home from Leipzig, I got an invitation to attend a Festival of Palestinian films in Baghdad, Iraq. At that time Iraq was considered America's worst enemy because of its leadership of the Arab world's opposition to the State of Israel, but I decided to accept the invitation nevertheless.

A free trip is a free trip, especially one going through both New York and London. I travelled on a British passport via London, and found myself in Baghdad just before Good Friday.

SITTING ON SADDAM HUSEIN'S PLATFORM

1977

To be in Iraq as a Rastawoman was a unique experience. Iraq was a very different country to any I had experienced before, with a different language and a very different culture. It was the first time I had seen men dressed in Arab headgear and clothing.

As a Rastawoman, my long skirt and covered head were perfectly in tune with the proper dress for women. Sadam had recently freed women from having to wear the long black shroud called an 'abaya' that Arab women used to cover themselves in, and allowed them to wear dresses with sleeves and skirts halfway below their knees. The women – and men – were grateful for this freedom to be 'modern'.

As a guest of the Iraq government, I had a chauffeur and a charming young female hostess and interpreter who went everywhere with me and who I assumed was also an undercover intelligence officer. I knew how controversial Iraq was, not just because of its support of the anti-Israel campaign, but also because of its oil wealth, so I was sure I was under surveillance to make sure that as the first Jamaican who had ever come to Iraq, I was not an enemy.

The city of Baghdad looked prosperous, with modern streets and buildings, busy people, happy faces. I was excited to be in a different culture with people wearing different dress and eating food cooked in new ways. The food was good with lots of humus and spiced vegetables, no pork anywhere on the menu in the restaurant of the lovely, modern hotel I was staying in overlooking the Bosphorus River.

Thanks to oil wealth, everyone had a job and a house, and the streets were calm and orderly with cars going to and fro about their business.

In the centre of Baghdad was an impressive monument gilded in gold leaf of Scherezade, the heroine of the well-known stories of the Thousand and One Arabian Nights in which a beautiful female captive saved her life by telling the Emperor a different story every night till he fell in love with her and cancelled her sentence of death. Baghdad honours her and is proud to be the city of the famous Arabian stories.

The market, or *soukh*, was filled with beautiful carpets, clothing and gold jewellery, with olives, honey, nuts and sweet deserts piled high on stalls. It was another world with items I had never seen before. I had been given an envelope of cash by my hostess when I arrived and I bought some gold and turquoise earrings, a small bedside carpet and some Palestinian scarves in the *soukh*.

In a downtown cinema the Festival showed films from around the world about the history of Palestine and Israel that explained and supported the Palestinian cause, some in English and some subtitled. There were lots of people attending from many Arab countries, speaking many languages and I became aware of being in a very politically important, revolutionary and dangerous place and time.

Among the VIP political guests were Yassir Arafat, head of the Palestinian Liberation Organization, and American pastor Jesse Jackson.

Among the activities there was a day trip to attend a celebration by the Kurdish people of northern Iraq, but I didn't go, staying instead to watch films. I later discovered I had missed a good opportunity to see these people who were fighting for independence from Iraq, and experience their culture. Another trip offered was to Babylon on Good Friday, but I didn't want to go there either, especially not on Good Friday.

Instead, accompanied by my guide and wearing a black 'abaya' over my long skirt and covered head, I spent an interesting few hours milling around in the courtyard of a large mosque with Muslims of many African countries and following the line of people dropping money and praying around the mausoleum of the saint buried there.

I felt happy embraced by the crowd of Africans of all nations, all Muslim. I was in good company. My hostess told me people were asking which African country I came from and when she told them Jamaica, they had never heard of my country.

The other two female guests at the film festival were the Italian sex symbol film star Gina Lollobrigida, who my hostess whispered was Saddam's girlfriend. She was still a major celebrity who had starred in a few Hollywood films, and she acted like she was Liz Taylor, decked in diamonds and a lot of expensive jewelery.

The other female guest was the renowned English classical actress and anti-Israel activist Vanessa Redgrave. She was a very major, outspoken and respected global celebrity who had jeopardized her career by supporting the Palestinian cause.

Soon after arrival I was taken in convoy with other guests and journalists to Saddam Hussein's palace where, after a long wait where our credentials were checked, we were ushered into a press conference with Saddam.

For some reason, I was given the chance to ask the first question, which I asked in full TV-journalist mode. I don't remember what I asked him and I realized afterwards that I knew so little about the man and his country that I should have declined and let someone else ask first. But he answered me graciously, like a father patting a child on the head.

Sometime after that I was taken to a TV studio to be interviewed. I wore my natural hair in an upswept bun that day, as an alternative to my Afro (those were the days before my locks), but shortly after doing the interview, my lady guide and interpreter brought me back from the hotel to do the interview again, asking would I please comb out my hair into an Afro again.

When I asked her why it had to be done again with my hair combed out, she said "So that Saddam can see you better." I did that and did the interview again.

On the final night of the film festival there was an entertainment event featuring a fashion show, which Miss Lollobrigida enjoyed with lots of loud cheers and applause, then a dinner party in a large hall. I was sitting with my interpreter when a man came to our table and said something which she interpreted to say that I was invited to sit on the platform with Saddam. I prepared to move up with my interpreter, but she said she was not invited.

Full of feminist indignation, I said I would not move unless she came with me and I remained seated, refusing to move. Knowing what I learned later about Saddam Hussein's autocracy and brutality, I can overstand why the hall fell silent and my interpreter observed me with some fear in her eyes, but I just stayed in my chair and the evening proceeded with her by my side.

Since then I have thought about how ungracious I was to have refused the President's invitation and chosen instead to stay with the 'common people'. Looking at the gold earrings and bracelet I bought in the Baghdad *soukh* with the ample pocket money I was given before I left Baghdad, I think more could have happened if I had accepted Saddam's invitation to sit closer.

Maybe – knowing I was returning penniless and jobless to Jamaica – sitting beside him may have given me a chance to invite him to invest economically in my future with some of his oil Dollar$$$. (Smile!) At the very least, I would now have a photo of me beside such a famous historic person.

But once when I told this story in my son's presence,

he said: "You would be dead by now Mom if you had sat on Saddam's platform."

I kinda think he's right, as I realize that my trips to Cuba, East Germany and Iraq had certainly put me on the USA's intelligence radar screen as a potential revolutionary and trouble-maker. We can now see how America's hatred of Iraq for its support of the Palestinian cause went to its highest point decades later with 9/11 and its aftermath.

It's no surprise to me that America finally found in 9/11 an excuse to invade and eliminate the largest and best-funded Arab support of the Palestinian cause in the fight against the State of Israel, even as time has shown that Iraq had nothing to do with 9/11.

But I received a vivid enough warning not to get too close to America's enemies. When I arrived at London airport on my way home from Baghdad, I found that my suitcase had been ripped apart and all my things scattered in a spiteful act of destruction against someone coming from Iraq. I could barely gather all my belongings together in the pieces of the broken suitcase and struggle to the Iraq Airlines counter.

But the Iraq Airlines staff just smiled and immediately gave me enough money to buy the largest, most expensive suitcase I wanted in one of the airport shops to replace it, sending a stewardess with me to make the purchase, leaving plenty of left over pocket money. It seems they were accustomed to such things happening to Western people who travelled to Iraq.

For years after that, the Iraq stamp in my passport

always assured me of a long in-transit delay and check by Immigration Control whenever I passed through the USA, and I was glad when that passport containing entry stamps from Cuba, East Germany and Iraq finally expired.

It's the same reason why I turned down an invitation years later from Nation of Islam minister Louis Farrakhan to visit Lybia and meet Gaddafi.

I had met Dr. Farrakhan when Muhammad Ali brought him to Jamaica in 1974 and I thought what he had to say was much more interesting than trying to meet Ali, as all other journalists had done. So I sat with him in his hotel room and interviewed him for a two-part article in the STAR newspaper.

We were still talking an hour later, when the adjoining room door opened and Muhammad Ali poked his head inside. "Don't you want to interview me too?" he smiled.

I was embarassed, because Farrahhan was more interesting, but Ali just smiled and said "That's why I brought him to Jamaica."

At the end of the interview Farrakhan gave me a copy of his book in which he had written *"To Barbara: Thanks for making my visit to Jamaica memorable"* and when he came to Jamaica several times after that, I made sure to attend his lectures and greet him.

But I had to think deeply about accepting his invitation to Lybia. Gaddafi was so controversial, even though it was long before he tried to set up an African currency based on the 460 tons of Gold held in Iraq's vault.

Much as I admired Gaddafi for his intention to liberate Africa from the power of the US Dollar, I'm very glad I didn't accept that invitation.

WORKING FOR THE CITY

My stop in London from Iraq was a good refresher for my friends the Jamaican actors Anton Phillips and his wife Judy, who had settled and become Londoners around the same time I had, and were (and still are) my 'family'. They had appointed me Godmother to their two beautiful daughters and wished I would come back to live in London.

A special guest at dinner one evening was Linton 'Kwesi' Johnson, just becoming famous for his revolutionary Black poetry. I was very impressed with him. This was the new Black London, Black Britain, nourished by Black Power and Black is Beautiful. I was glad to see its existence.

But no way was I coming back to England. I was going back home.

I stopped in New York at the invitation of a leading Jamaican woman I had met in the highest political circles.

"You can stay with me," she had offered. It was a good opportunity to visit Rhea, a White American girlfriend who wanted me to meet a producer she thought would be interested in the film script I carried with me, my version of Bob Marley's song *"I Shot The Sherrif"*.

Meeting him over lunch, to prove his qualifications he introduced me to one of his clients, the author Ntozake Shange whose play *"For Coloured Girls Who Have*

Considered Suicide When The Rainbow Is Not Enuf" was the top show on Broadway. I spent an afternoon enjoying a matinee performance of the play and drinks afterwards with Ntozake, but the producer soon made it clear that any help from him for my script came at a sexual price I was not interested in paying.

Back at the Jamaican woman's apartment, it also became plainly clear that her invitation was to share not just her apartment, but her bed – another price I was not interested in paying. I slept an uncomfortable night on her couch.

I have nothing against homosexuality. I have always had a few 'gay' friends and it is always obvious that there are many male homosexuals occupying the heights of Jamaican power, especially in media and entertainment. But this was the first lesbian I had ever met, and I was definitely not interested in that side of the sexual equation. But she was powerful enough that I did not want to offend her directly.

In a panic, I called Rhea. "Come over," she said. Her apartment was a mirrored boudoir specially decorated for visits from her man – who she later married – not suitable for visiting Jamaican girlfriends. But she had a solution.

"You need a massage. You need to meet Bill, " she said, calling a friend then sending me by taxi to a space shared by healers offering different kinds of therapies. I received a good professional massage from Bill – a really nice Black man whose soft touch and wise words were just what I needed after Baghdad, London, the New York producer and the Jamaican lesbian.

I agreed to meet him later that evening for dinner and a movie. He took me to Benihanna, the Chinese restaurant in Manhattan where the chefs make a show of cooking your dinner at your table, then we went to see the film "*A Married Woman*" which made me feel guilty about the boyfriend back home in Jamaica.

When the film was over he hired a taxi and told the driver "Through the Park" and I had the pleasure of a romantic drive through Central Park at night to a brownstone house in Harlem where his aunt was delighted to welcome me to her home.

I didn't have to think twice about where I preferred to sleep that night.

*

Coming back home to Jamaica from Iraq in 1979, I was even more committed as a Pan-African, pro-Cuba revolutionary.

Hearing that President Jose Eduardo dos Santos of Angola, still fighting its revolutionary war against Portugese colonialism, was stopping in Jamaica on his way to speak at the UN, I made sure to be at his press conference at the Jamaica Pegasus hotel in my capacity as a free-lance (unemployed) journalist. I was a big supporter of the African wars of anti-colonial liberation and Angola was a major war that Cuba was assisting in the usual way Fidel Castro helped and supported them all.

The established media soon ran out of questions for

this not-so-famous African leader whose war they clearly knew little about, so I raised my hand. "Mr. President, I would like to give you the opportunity to defend the presence of Cuban soldiers in Angola."

The President was both surprised and happy for my intervention and glad to take the opportunity to speak directly on the matter. He explained the colonial history of Portugal in Angola and gave the reasons why he was grateful that Cuban soldiers were helping the Angolan guerilla army to fight the long and bitter battle for independence. I saw the journalists quickly making notes so they could use his comments in their stories.

When I got home later, I received a call from the Ministry of Foreign Affairs informing me that the Angolan President was very grateful for my question at the Press Conference and wanted to meet with me at the airport on his way back from the UN. On the appointed day an official car drove me to the airport, where the Minister of Foreign Affairs, the Cuban Ambassador and President dos Santos awaited.

Surrounded by Jamaican police and Ministry officials, we spoke in Spanish. I gave him a copy of that week's TIME Magazine, which had a large feature on several African revolutionary wars, and a casette tape with Pablo Moses reggae song *"We Should Be In Angola"*. As time came for him to leave, he asked the Cuban Ambassador to arrange to fly me to Angola as a journalist to write about the war. It sounded like a good idea to me.

But as we stood on the tarmac watching him walk to the waiting jet, the plane revved its engines and a blast of very hot air hit us, the hottest heat I had ever experienced. As I retreated from the fiery heat, it seemed like an instant warning from JAH of what awaited me if I accepted that invitation, a sign that I should not go to Angola. When the Cuban Embassy contacted me later, I turned down the offer.

Obeying that warning was a good decision. Dos Santos turned out to be a bad leader, and I would have had a very bad personal experience. Reading this year about his daughter Isobel dos Santos, now allegedly 'the richest Black woman in Africa' who is accused of appropriating billions of Angola's Dollars in financial crimes, I recall the revolutionary support I had of President Dos Santos and shake my head with astonishment.

It's sad that the battle we Pan-Africanists had supported with our hearts and minds so many decades ago to put the mineral resources of Angola in Black African hands, has had such a shocking turn in modern times.

Who could have thought things would turn out the way they have!!!

*

I realised it was time for me to stop trying to be a revolutionary and try to become a GOOD GIRL. Instead of going to Angola, I decided to look for a job.

A friend told me that the Kingston & St. Andrew Corporation was advertising for a Public Relations Officer. I had earned my PR qualifications from the Institute of Public

Relations when I lived in London and worked at the fancy London PR company that Jamaica used for Tourism-and-government matters. I also had my qualifications as PRO for *"The Harder They Come"*. I was qualified, so I applied and was called for an interview. I removed my head-wrap, combed out my hair that was still not locksed, and put on my best Uptown outfit.

The KSAC was not a highly-regarded government organization. Second in power to the national Parliament, it was a mini-government of Councillors representing various sectors and services of the City. But it was considered a scorpions nest of politics, so its reputation meant there were only two of us waiting in the lobby to be interviewed.

The other person, a man, suddenly got up and left. He later said that when he saw me he realised he would not get the job, so he went off and wrote a play that became a big success.

I got the job.

The KSAC ran the 17 divisions of the City of Kingston with a large staff spread out over the city handling such services as road repairs, garbage collection, social housing, care for the poor, and also civic functions. It was a daily political hotbed, as the decisions to run the City were made by the Councillors elected in each Division who met each day to discuss various aspects of work. There was always a quarrel about something or other, as the Councillors competed fiercely against each other for benefits for their constituencs – and themselves.

The Mayor and all but two of the Councillors were PNP, the ruling government Party, while the two JLP councillors were constant victims of hostility, rage and even fighting. Staff were also divided along Party lines and we were not expected to have good relations with the JLP Councillors. I didn't care and spoke equally to all of them, even though some of the more die-hard politicos frowned to see me doing that.

To top it off, my job had been previously been done, incompetently, by a man who still remained in his post and office, though the title and, ostensibly, power had been shifted to me. I did my best to implement some proper Public Relations for the City, despite his constant effort to undermine me and curtail my efforts.

The gravy train of the department was the hiring of the KSAC stage by people wanting to present events. He controlled the stage rentals and I eventually had to simply turn a deaf ear and blind eye to anything to do with stages and the funds he collected for renting them out.

Instead as there was little good news about the KSAC to put out as public relations releases, I decided instead to use PR to raise the morale of the workers.

I proposed a Clean City Cat PR campaign, with the Ward Theatre as our logo, working with Ruby Martin, the beautiful wife of the Custos of St. Andrew who was determined to bring the historic theatre back to functioning use. We created Clean City Cat T-shirts for all the Public Cleansing workers to wear and arranged for us to be photographed presenting one to Prime Minister Manley.

I invited each of the KSAC's departments to select a pretty girl to be their 'Queen' for a Miss KSAC competition, then arranged for each department to make a float for their candidate to parade through the city on a bright Saturday. There was one stream of floats beginnning in the west of the city at the Public Cleansing Department, one stream coming from Rockfort Gardens in the east, and a central parade from Half Way Tree to the waterfront downtown, each led by marching bands and uniformed cadets, Scouts and Girl Guides.

It was a huge success. Seventeen floats carrying the departments' queens accompanied by marching bands paraded through the streets of Kingston, drawing crowds and creating happiness across the City. In the evening the Miss KSAC contestants were hosted at the Mayor's residence and a Queen crowned. It was all a huge success.

I was proud to have organized an event that upgraded the image of the KSAC in such a major way. The Clean City Cat campaign, the float parade, and especially the Miss KSAC Contest made the citizens of Kingston realise that the organization that took care of everything that kept the capital running, was staffed by people like themselves, people who actually tried their best to do a good job, not just the quarelling politicians that used to be all they heard about the KSAC. I felt I had justified my employment fully.

In another PR idea, I proposed that the Keys to the City be awarded to three Jamaicans: singer and actor Harry

Belafonte whose song '*Jamaica Farewell*' was wel known; the beloved actor and comedian Ranny Williams, who had been making us laugh on stages and radio programmes for years, and Bob Marley who was already the island's most popular music artist.

The proposal was sent to Jamaica House where my former boss, the Minister for Culture, responded with approval for Belafonte and Williams, but refused to include Marley. "He would have to cut his hair and stop smoking ganja," was the reply sent back to the PR department.

The refusal presented a problem because I had gone to Bob first and told him that I had proposed him as a recipient of the Keys and asked him if he would accept them.

"Me want to bu'n down Babylon," he said, "but since is you ask me Barbara, I will do it."

Now I was faced with the embarassment of telling Bob what the decision had been. But Bob just laughed and went back into the studio where he was laying tracks and finding lyrics for the song "*I'm A Black Survivor*".

"*Some have plans and schemes, some have hopes and dreams,*" were the lyrics.

'Never mind Barbara. Babylon mus' burn," was Bob's last word.

Harry Belafonte had scheduling conflicts and declined the KSAC invitation to the planned gala presentation. Ranny Williams, the beloved old man who had played the role of Santa every year at the KSAC's Children's Christmas Party and who had been entertaining Jamaica for years in the annual Pantomime, especially in collaboration with "Miss Lou" Louise Bennett, was in hospital having his diabetic leg removed. I gathered together some of the KSAC's pretty ladies, bought a huge bunch of flowers and we surprised Uncle Ranny with a visit that I know warmed his heart.

Despite these PR activities that had brought some shine to the KSAC's dull and criticised reputation, I remained 'on probation' in the job for a year. When at the end of a year the Town Clerk Keith Miller proposed that my probationary period continue still longer, I felt it was time to say goodbye to the KSAC and its unpleasant people.

I had been trying to get pregnant by the man I had been living with for several years, but he said I was 'barren'. The doctor examining me said I had 'growths', ovarian cysts that had to be moved as they were preventing impregnation. This seemed a good time to have that operation, so I declined the KSAC's invitation to endure another period of 'probation' and left to have the operation.

The lady doctor who performed the operation said there were so many ovarian cysts inside my womb that had to be removed, she wanted to do a hysterectomy, but she had done her best because she knew I wanted a child. When the wound re-opened a week after I was sent home and I had to be re-admitted for a blood transfusion, I read through the Book of St. Luke, the physician, as two pints of blood were pumped into me. It took several weeks for me to recover.

I later learned that use of lye-based chemical hair straighteners has been proved to cause ovarian cysts, and that

Black women are the major victims. As one of the first women to use the lye-based products when they were introduced and having been using them for at least 10 years, it was no wonder my womb was populated by the growths. It was a miracle, a real miracle that I got pregnant many years later.

In a final vicious act, the KSAC siezed the motor car it had insisted I purchase with a loan from them and some of my salary savings. Now that I had resigned, they insisted on me returning the loan immediately and while I lay in bed in a house on the hilly back roads of Red Hills recovering from such a major operation, they seized the car, put it on sale in a friendly car mart and when the sale was completed, told me they only raised enough money to cover their loan to me, not the amount I had also invested in it to meet the purchase price.

JAH does not sleep. A few weeks later the KSAC official who had supervised the sale of my car was held up at his gate, robbed of his car, and shot dead.

Stuck up in the mountains with no transportation or income while I rested and healed, I decided it was time to look outside Jamaica again.

Barbara Gloudon, the progressive editor of the daily STAR newspaper who noticed me coming in to the GLEANER offices regularly selling my free-lance articles, asked me to write five articles on Rastafari. It was a very good offer I was glad to receive.

Regretting having left the Rastafari path to take the KSAC job, writing the articles was something good to do as I healed and so I did my best in writing to explain as much as I could and as best I could about the path I was following.

I was pleased when Barbara Gloudon published the articles one a day over five days in her popular paper, and when I went to the GLEANER's office a week later to buy copies, I found that the paper had sold out on four of the five days of publication.

I realised that if the articles were that popular, there was an interest in the information shared by someone active in the faith, and I could see that the articles had the potential to be expanded into a book. All I needed to do was add some more details and information.

So with that in mind, I set off down the path of becoming an author.

REMEMBER THE COPTICS

I had some good help to start me on the road as an author. My articles had been noticed elsewhere. A good friend told me that he had received instructions to bring me to meet the Coptics, a group of Jamaicans whose community had been joined by hippie-type White Americans and evolved into what they called a new Rastafari mansion. The Coptics had been publishing a free newspaper in which they promoted the legalization of ganja and distributed it island-wide via one of the many trucks whose drivers had become part of the Coptic business and they had published two of my articles in issues of the paper.

The Coptics business was ganja and over the years they became rich and notorious from ganja. The Americans found innovative ways of getting ganja from Jamaica to America by sea and air, as some of them had been pilots in the US VietNam war which gave them valuable skills for moving ganja. They were good with boats too.

Everyone knew what the Coptics were doing, though few knew exactly how they did it. Everyone wanted them to be successful, because their success was bringing economic benefits to many Jamaicans in the Seventies through ganja, so they were glad that the Coptics headed a quiet ganja revolution across the island of growers and transporters.

We went to visit the Coptics, driving some distance east of Kingston to St. Thomas and then inland, up a long road to a big house on a big property. The main focus of the property was a beautiful 12-sided tabernacle with wooden louvre doors and a roof painted Red, Gold and Green. I could hear prayers being chanted inside.

On the grounds were several houses and buildings where the Coptic people lived. There were men and women, Black and White, moving around the property on which there were many cars and some large agricultural equipment and machinery.

In a large upstairs room Niah Keith Gordon – the Jamaican leader of the Coptics - sat on a beautifully carved throne-like chair upholstered in red velvet. Seated on a similar chair beside him was Brother Louv, a tall, thin white man with long hair and long beard who was the chief White Coptic. Around the room sat several men, Black and White, dressed in Red, Gold and Green robes and wearing long beards, but no locks. I learned later that the beautiful carved furniture was one of the ways the Coptics moved ganja out of Jamaica.

I could hear more prayers being said, Psalms being chanted and there was lots of ganja being smoked in clay pipes, rather than spliffs. A huge pile of ganja sat on a table in the middle of the room, the biggest amount I had ever seen at one time. Someone put some in my hands with a spliff paper and I rolled one. A stick from the fire was brought for me to light it and I relaxed and inhaled some very good ganja.

The Coptics said they asked to meet me because they wanted to thank me for the articles I had been writing about ganja and its legalization. They showed me copies of their *Coptic Times* newspaper in which they had reprinted my articles, and I was proud at the notice. It was the first meeting with the Coptic brethren and I spent a long day there talking with everyone, including the women.

I was given a tour of the residential quarters and saw several unoccupied, beautifully furnished rooms and rooms, any of which would have made me a comfortable residence. I realised there was an unspoken invitation for me to join them if I wanted. Living as I did on the edge of poverty, it was a tempting offer.

However, I saw that they lived a communal lifestyle and that joining them would mean cutting myself off from the independent life I was presently living. I also didn't think I would be comfortable around so many White people, who seemed to be the ones in charge.

There was something I couldn't accept about the Coptics too. They did not love Emperor Haile Selassie. The Coptics gave all praise and honour to Marcus Garvey, but they promoted in their paper Garveys criticism of the Emperor who, Garvey said, left Ethiopia like a coward and stayed in England as a British puppet during the Italian invasion. These comments by Garvey were written long before he and the world could realise the wisdom of the Emperor's appeal to Britain for military help, which led to to the successfull victory by Ethiopia of Italy's effort to colonise it. Garvey certainly regretted his words after that, but they remain a blot on Garvey's record.

Every Rasta Mansion has its own special form of dogma and the Coptics version was not mine, but I was quite comfortable in their company because of their brave support of ganja for personal and national economic benefit. I definitely agreed with them and the bold way they were fighting that revolution.

I told Niah Keith that I was thinking of selling my typewriter to earn the fare to leave Jamaica and publish my first book in New York. He told me that if I did, I should stop in Miami at their Star Island home and meet the Coptics there. I certainly wanted to write an article about them that I was sure a newspaper would pay me for, and it would be interesting to meet their Miami counterparts, so it was set.

I sold my typewriter and bought a ticket to Miami, not knowing what I would do from there on, but trusting in JAH to take care of me. I had an aunt in Orlando and in my bag were the STAR articles that I knew could become a book with which I could earn enough to live on. With that optimism, I left Jamaica.

Star Island was an island of luxury residences that was connected to Miami by boat and an over-sea highway. The Coptics lived in a large house and the life there was just as I had seen it in Jamaica, with lots of people living together, moving around, eating, cooking, talking, praying, smoking. I spent three days there talking with them, reading the books and papers in their library, gathering material for my article and enjoying being in the company of ganja smokers with an endless supply.

When it came time to depart, Sister Louv, the wife of the leading Coptic man Brother Louv, gave me with a brown paper bag like the ones patties are sold in that was as heavy as if a patty was inside. "Niah Keith said to give you this."

A patty from Niah Keith! I looked inside and was shocked to see that its weight was caused by the pile of Hundred Dollar bills it contained. Sister Louv just smiled. "Just call us when you need more," she said.

Now I had my plane fare to New York, and enough money to rent a nice apartment while I finished my book, plus the security of knowing that I could call on the Coptics if and when I needed more money. It was a great beginning and I headed to New York with thanks to the Coptics, and a smile.

Through my girlfriend Rhea, I found a lovely apartment in the Central Park West complex uptown New York at 94th Street, a nice neighbourhood not too far from Harlem. With the money in my patty bag, I bought a new typewriter and a ream of paper, then sat down at the window and started writing new chapters to fill up the book.

I enjoyed being in New York. I had passed through the City a few times and knew my around the subways, but this time I was on my own with enough money to buy food, pay rent and live on my own schedule. I started exploring the city and my neighbourhood. The apartment was near Central Park and in a neighbourhood with good shops and food stores. There was a lot that remained of the days when

Harlem was the center of Black American culture and
politics.

There was a lot to remind me of Black American
politics too. I remember being at a huge rally held to welcome
Robert Mugabe to New York, after he had become Black
Africa's superstar leader for winning the war against White
Rhodesia and its racist leader Ian Smith and re-naming his
country Zimbabwe. People were proud to remind me that
Fidel Castro had stayed in Harlem when he came to address
the United Nations.

Shops, restaurants and music stores advertised pieces
of Black history that they sold and it was as if the
neighbourhood was a living museum where people walked
around in an air of past glory and present hope.

On one of my trips up to Harlem, I saw a fruit stall on
the corner of 125th Street that had a Red, Black and Green flag
of Marcus Garvey flying on one corner. An old man dressed in
a Garveyite uniform was standing beside it, selling the fruit.

Who are you? I asked him. Do you know about
Marcus Garvey?

The old man laughed heartily.

"I was Garvey's bodyguard," the old man said. "I am
one of Garvey's cubs."

What do you mean, I asked.

The answer I got was the start of one of my most
amazing friendships of my life. He was Captain James
Thornhill and the fruit stall was his. He was one of the few
remaining officers of the UNIA and had been close to Mr.

Garvey all his life, and still upholding the Red, Black and Green banner that flew on the corner of his stall.

With a crisp salute, Captain Thornhill said when Mr. Garvey was alive he had accompanied Mr. Garvey wherever he went. He told me that Mr. Garvey had once said "You may kill me, but my cubs are alive!" He said he was one of Garvey's cubs.

Captain Thornhill became my 'father' in New York while I was writing the book, always full of stories of Marcus Garvey and the glorious history of that time. I visited him often, at the fruit stall and at his home, where I met his wife and daughter. Once he took me with him to Philadelphia to a meeting of old Garveyites and I spent a day listening to their stories about my National Hero.

Captain Thornill would tell me annecdotes about Mr. Garvey and the adventures he had with him. I loved being in his company. He was a treasure trove of information for a writer who loved Marcus Garvey so much, and he was a perfect companion when I wanted human communication.

Captain Thornhill also introduced me to Dr. Josef Ben Jochanan, the leading Black scholar of Egyptology and author of the book "*Africa – The Mother of all World Religions*" and several other books of Black history and knowledge.

Dr. Ben not only added to my education, but he showed me how to produce my book the same way he self-published his own books, so that I could have them printed in a simple and inexpensive operation. I typed out each page and assembled the book, designed a cover and I was able to publish the first edition of my new book "*Rastafari – The New Creation*" and put it on the street in 1979, thanks to Dr. Ben's publishing advice and help.

Copies sold well because there was little information about Rastafari at that time and it was the first book on Rasta that had been written by a Rasta. Thanks to the Coptics, I had no financial worries and I was happy with life.

I presented a copy to the director of the Schomberg, where I had spent many hours researching Garvey and enjoying the Museum's treasures. It was at the Schomberg that I first heard Garvey's voice on a tape recording of one of his speeches.

I was now an author!

I was so proud to have achieved that milestone!

I give unceasing thanks to the Coptics who made my dream a reality.

But as winter approached the weather was cold and depressing, so I decided to return to Jamaica with a few copies of my book to sell.

Looking at that edition today, I have to smile at how simple and basic it was. Letter-size pages, typewitten in big letters and with a few photos scattered within. It was very basic, but it was a book! MY book!!!

*   *   *   *

One thing I did when I got home was arrange to bring Captain Thornhill to Jamaica to fulfill his dream of seeing the country where his hero Marcus Garvey was born. I wrote an article about him "*Garvey's Cubs*" and when it was published the Coptics were glad to buy a ticket for him and to meet him.

Ocho Rios music producer Jack Ruby was so impressed to meet Captain Thornhill, that he placed his Mercedes Benz car and driver at our disposal to show the old man around Garvey's hometown St. Anns Bay to see the house where he was born, the statue outside the Parish Library that I had helped unveil, and the beautiful Parish of St. Ann. I was so glad to have done something nice for Captain Thornhill.

New York was the start of my career as an author.

HOLLYWOOD AGAIN

1981

Home again, I soon ran out of printed copies. To finance a second printing, I went to Chris Blackwell. He took one look at the cover and told one of his minions "Give her what she needs." Thanks Chris.

I printed the second edition and tried to interest bookshops and stores to buy and distribute them, but my informal printing method was not as attractive to them as the paperback romance novels with their glossy colour covers. Rastas were not interested in buying. They either had no money, or felt that since it was 'about them' they should receive free copies.

Just as I was getting frustrated with Jamaica again, Vonetta called and invited me to visit her again in Los Angeles. I was very glad to accept and she sent me a ticket.

Vonetta was still living in the same property with the big house we had painted with pine oil, but the living arrangements were very different. Vonetta and Max were no longer a couple. I never asked for or got details of why, but I accepted that was the reality.

Max alone now occupied the big house, living like a

hermit recluse that no one ever saw. Vonetta was living in the 2-bedroom guest house at the end of the long driveway. She gave me a bedroom there overlooking the snow-capped mountains and was glad of my company.

Max wanted Vonetta to move out off the property, and Vonetta was determined to continue living there as she was co-owner. Neither of them spoke to each other. Both were fighting for sole control and residency of the property, and the legal battle was fierce. Vonetta also had a new man, a big music executive producer of Stevie Wonder's music, and it created even more conflict with Max when her boyfriend drove up the driveway in his mink coat and Rolls Royce to see her.

Vonetta spent a lot of time and money with expensive lawyers in expensive Los Angeles offices. At the same time she was doing a lot to stay healthy, as she was just recovering from her second bout of breast cancer. She was the first person I knew who drank spirulina for its health benefits and she was on a strict vegan diet. It wasn't a happy time of her life, and I was glad to be keeping her company while she tried to survive and win. But I told her she was making a mistake just giving all her hard-earned money to lawyers and advised her to cut her losses, marry the music producer and move on.

I tried to sell copies of my books, but what I earned didn't help me buy my own food to put in Vonetta's health-food-filled fridge. There had to be a solution.

Just when I thought JAH had completely forgotten about me, I was sitting one cold morning looking out the window when a little bird flew up and rested on a branch. Soon another little bird joined the first one, then a third. I smiled as I remembered Bob Marley's song *'Three Little Birds'* and my spirits lifted.

Just as the song came to an end in my mind, I got a call from Roger Steffens, a Los Angeles journalist and collector of Bob Marley reggae memorabilia, inviting me to a screening of some footage that might become a movie about reggae. When he asked me how things were, I confessed they weren't good as I was broke and I was hoping to get to England, where I felt sure there was a publisher for my book.

My miracles always surprise me and this one happened at just the right time. Out of his enormous heart, Roger arranged for the film's production budget to buy me a ticket to London. I said thanks and farewell to Vonetta, wishing her luck in her property and the emotional woes that I couldn't help.

I don't know how the house and Max worked out, but she eventually found a lovely husband in the Black actor Carl Lumley and had a son with him. He starred in a TV series set in Jamaica and they bought a beautiful beach house in Port Maria. She had a son with Carl and and I visited them there once when my son Makonnen was four. I was glad our sons met each other and to see her happiness with Carl. We spent a lovely day together.

Sadly, Vonetta died two years ago. Newspapers, online stories and film magazines paid tribute to her work as a major Hollywood movie star and some of her movies were released.

It's hard to believe that my great friend Vonetta is no longer around. She had shown me such a beautiful and unusual part of life that I will never forget and I hope my few words here pay some tribute to the wonderful person she was. Vonetta's beauty and her loveliness is captured forever in her films and in the hearts of all like me who love her.

Sad but true, Hollywood is just like the movies.

LONDON ONCE AGAIN

Anton Phillips and his wife Judy, the Jamaican actors, were kind enough to put me up at their home again. I got to meet their two young daughters who were as beautiful as their mother, and I had been appointed their Godmother when they each were born, so it was good to get to see them again, now they were six and seven years old.

I called up an old friend Jeremy Isaacs, who had been the Programme Director at THAMES TV when I got the job on the *"Today"* show that made me famous. He had been powerless to stop the *"Today"* producer from not renewing my contract, but we had remained friends and he often invited me to dinner parties with his wife at his home.

Jeremy was glad I was in London again and invited me to lunch. He was now heading a brand new television station starting up, CHANNEL 4-UK, that was set up to provide alternative television programming for minority and underserved communities.

It had been ten years since we last met and Jeremy was surprised to see I was a different person. No more short, straightened hair, no make-up. Instead, a natural hairstyle covered in a wrap. No trousers, but a flared skirt. An unusual person, a Rastawoman.

As we talked I told Jeremy about my spiritual and

racial beliefs that were responsible for the person I was, and
that prevented me from living happily in England's racism
any longer. I told him I was surprised that ten years after I
had become the first Black TV journalist, there had not been a
flourishing of jobs for Black journalists and serious
programmes for the Black communities.

I criticized the British media for not using its powers
of print, television and show business to break down the
barriers of racism that seemed just as high ten years later as
they had been when I left. I said it was a shame that so much
racism still existed and I was glad to know he was heading a
channel that was intended to be doing something to change
racist attitudes.

As he listened, Jeremy had an idea.

"I would like you to make a film for Channel Four
about your view of England ten years after leaving."

What a great idea! What a great opportunity! I was
glad to be invited to put my comments on film.

Jeremy put me in touch with a Commissioning Editor
who would supervise my production and provide the budget
for me. He knew I knew enough about television production
to be able to make a film and was happy to put the project in
motion.

My first job was to put together a crew. I wanted to
use an all-Black crew because I was going to make some very
Black statements and needed a crew who would not be critical
or prejudiced against my views. I had to apply specially to the
film makers union for this permission, which had never

previously been granted, but eventually I received permission.

However, there weren't enough Black film makers to fill all the posts. No Black director, so I hired a White female director who used to work with me on the *"Today"* show. I was glad to find a Jamaican cameraman, and as film editor I found a Trinidadian-Indian whose work putting the film together in the editing room became the most important contribution to the production. I found two young Black trainees and a Jamaican sound man who recommended a White lighting technician who did an excellent job.

I selected my interview subjects carefully. I interviewed my friend Tessa Topolski, whose father was a renowned society artist at whose home important people in the arts and politics would gather. It was there that I met both Princess Margaret and Michael X at the same party. I was friends with her brother Daniel and she liked me, but she thought it was crazy of me to have gone back to Jamaica and become a Rasta.

I interviewed Anton about what being a Black actor was like and being a Black father of young children. I interviewed a group of Black women about the problems women had living in a racist Britain.

I interviewed Joan Bakewell, whom I consider the best TV journalist Britain has ever known (she has now been made a Dame by the Queen, justifiably), and tackled her about the failure of the traditional media to help erase the source of racism. I spoke with Arif Ali, a Guyanese publisher whose newspaper 'Caribbean Times' was a vociferous advocate of Black rights, and to which I was contributing a weekly column.

I interviewed Chauncey Huntley, musician and member of Ras Messengers – a Nyabinghi group whose music I featured in the film, and whose parents ran a Black bookshop and who, nevertheless, disapproved of him being a Rasta.

I filmed some scenes in Birmingham, where MP Enoch Powell's racism had been so great that no hotel would rent me a room when I worked at ATV studios ten years earlier, forcing me to commute daily between there and London. What surprised me about Birmingham ten years later was how many of the young born-there Blacks who were children when I worked there, were all now teenagers becoming Rasta with dreadlocks, clothing style and attitude – clearly their Black reaction, like mine, to the racism they lived with.

Island Films allowed me to use a clip from *"The Harder They Come'* of Jimmy Cliff and Ras Daniel Heartman over the song *"Sitting In Limbo"*. Ras Messengers and I-JahMan Levi allowed me to use music from their albums for the soundtrack.

To close the film, I returned to my old neighbourhood and strolled down Portobello Road, Notting Hill, where I used to shop weekly for Jamaican food and antique clothing. There, in a playground, I found a racially-mixed group of children whose happy play together showed what the future could be.

My film *'Race, Rhetoric, Rastafari'* was shown in the opening months of CHANNEL FOUR-TV and remains a much-praised and much-viewed 4-part documentary to be seen on YouTube.

I was proud to have added 'Film Director" to my bio again, but back home again in Jamaica, Paul Bucknor and Johnny Ghisays – the co-directors of JBC-TV, our only TV station – were not interested in showing my film.

"Too much Rasta," was their refusal.

Sigh!

I knew my film was good, but even more, it was showing the controversial topic of Rastafari in a positive light. I knew it was as good as, if not much better than anything anyone in Jamaica had done in recent times. It was also history that a Jamaican, and a woman, had made a documentary with a Jamaican cultural viewpoint that had been screened all over Britain in 1983. That alone gave a good reason to show my film.

But the highest heights of power at JBC were held by men opposed to me not only as a Rasta, but as a woman. All the heights of Jamaican media and culture at that time were occupied by men who had little use for women, men who had been carefully selected and mentored in their posts by the biggest misoginist of them all. Those gender blocks remained in place for many, many years, some even to today.

'Race, Rhetoric, Rastafari' is now online at YouTube. Have a look!

NO MORE RASTA!

The relationship with the man I had been living with for 9 years ended when I got back to Jamaica from making the film in London, and found that he had moved on. His main reason: I was 'too Rasta".

The new girl he had moved into the flat we had lived in was young, wore lipstick and tight pants.

Hmmm.

Being 'Rasta' was nothing 'worthy' in his eyes.

I was homeless too.

I packed up my few remaining things in another suitcase and caught a bus up into the hills to the only friend I could think of, who drove a truck bringing marketwomen into town on Thursday nights. As I sat in the truck in that long night waiting for it to be filled with marketwomen and their baskets and hoping he could help me find somewhere to live, I did a lot of thinking about what being Rasta meant.

Had it really been a wise decision to devote my life to an unorthodox religion and a controversial way of life?

What had been the benefit?

I couldn't find the answers.

There was more sad news:

My friend Bob Marley died.

I hadn't seen him since the night I had to tell him the KSAC refused to give him the Keys to the City, and I was kinda ashamed to go and visit him after that. There were a lot of new people around Bob and with all the American journalists coming and going and writing about him in their glossy magazines, my work as a journalist writing in Jamaican newspapers was not needed.

It wasn't Bob who said that. I never got close enough to him any more, stopped by the human barrier of faces that frowned to see me and backs of bodies that shielded him from lesser mortals like me.

I didn't go to Bob's funeral. Watched it on TV instead. There didn't seem much point in adding to the crowd, many of whom Bob would have classified as 'hypocrites and parasites'. Rasta don't go a no man' funeral.

Bob's passing was a very big deal in Jamaica. The service at the National Arena was choreographed as a national event, with competition for influence from the Ethiopian Orthodox Church into which he had been baptized shortly before his death, and the Twelve Tribes of Israel Mansion that wanted the glory of saying he belonged to them. Their presence in the front row of the audience wearing full white with identical red, gold and green tams, certainly made them visible.

Rita, the widow, surrounded by the children, held the front row space, her head bowed under an Ethiopian scarf. In a few days she would forge Bob's signature and hand over all Bob's musical rights to Chris Blackwell's Island Records. She, and Bob's children, could say nothing when Blackwell later sold Island Records to a bigger record company, leaving them with very little of the million$ that would have been completely theirs if she hadn't done that.

Archbishop Yesehaq did his best to keep things going according to Ethiopian Orthodox Church ritual, but he acknowledged the Nyabinghi Rastafari element of Bob's life and let it be part of the service also. He said the prayers in Amharic, waved his censer of fragrant incense to purify the space, and held his processional cross high.

Meanwhile, the politicians and VIP filled other rows, pretending they had always known and loved the 'dutty Rasta', shocked to see that his funeral was larger and more popular than any of theirs would ever be.

The procession behind Bob's coffin across Jamaica to St. Ann was a motorcade never before seen in Jamaica. It seemed like every single Jamaican had made his or her way to a vantage point along the 40 miles of roads from Kingston. Politicians looked on with envy at a public homage they knew they would never get.

It was the funeral of a holy man, a superstar, a Rasta Man. It confirmed for us Rastas that what Bob represented – his locks, his profession of Selassie I, his ganja smoking, his reggae music, were all the BEST and GREATEST things to be in Jamaica and, in fact, the world.

Bob's funeral made all us Rastas proud to be RASTA.

But after Bob died, to my surprise, people turned to new musical styles. The people found new musical heroes to worship whose music was completely opposite to Bob's and instead of the spiritual hymns of reggae, the dancehall slackness of Yellow Man and Shabba Ranks topped the hit parade and even won Grammys.

I was very surprised the Rasta dream had not been strong enough to outlive Bob.

Why?

I looked around at 'Rasta' and saw a lot that wasn't right.

A lot of people not living up to the true principles .

A lot of people living opposite to the principles.

I couldn't identify with many of them.

What kind of Rasta was I? I had to ask myself.

I was a Rasta who lived by the CHRISTian principles outlined in the Bible, who lived the Ethiopian Orthodox way that was taught to me by Archbishop Yesehaq who was sent to Jamaica as Abba Mandefro by His Imperial Majesty, Emperor Haile Selassie I, Defender of the Holy Orthodox Faith, to teach Rastafari the way forward.

THAT was the Rasta I was, I am. Defined ONLY as one who follows the Ethiopian Orthodox pathway revealed by the actions of HIM who I&I worship as Divine.

A Rasta who believes in trying to do and be all and everything that the Emperor does that makes us see him as

Divine, because it is HIM that has guided I&I on this Right, Righteous CHRISTian pathway to Godliness.

A Rasta who believes that such a Man who had guided so many of I&I to see the CHRIST way of LIFE, is indeed Divine and worthy of utmost Honour, RASpect and Worship.

To be called just a 'Rasta' was an incomplete definition, without such an added explanation. Too many were adopting the title "Rasta" who did not live the Rastafari way.

"Don't call me just a 'Rasta'," I wrote.

"Call me a Rastafari Ethiopian Orthodox CHRISTian."

I wrote about all that in a Letter to the Editor of the GLEANER, Mr. Hector Wynter.

Mr Wynter used it as the Cover Story and center-spread of the Sunday Magazine, laid it out with photos and then created a very misleading headline:

"No more Rasta for me" says Barbara Blake".

Mr. Wynter's headline made it the most notorious and most hated article I had ever had published. Few people read it, most only heard of the headline. To this day some people judge me by a claim they have heard that I once said I wasn't a Rasta.

One man hated me so much he spent a lot of time blocking many things I was trying to do, because pasted on the wall when he was being checked into the General Penitentiary to serve a sentence for Fraud, was my article in which I criticized those 'Rastas' who were committing crimes and giving the movement a bad reputation in many ways.

It was hard trying to explain it all, or to endure the hatred that was aimed at me from Nyabinghi drums and voices all over the Rastafari Diaspora. It was one of the times when I wished JAH hadn't given me the work to write things that needed to be said.

I realise now that my article was a kind of 'The Emperor Has No New Clothes" story. It dared to say that Rastafari had become a pretense of what it claimed to be, not what the original creators had intended it be. My article unintentionallyy and unfortunately held up a picture of what it had become.

Perhaps I had hoped speaking out about it, like the child who said the emperor was naked, would make all the bad bits fall off, diisappear, go away and leave the orginal form that Rastas like Dougie Mack and Marcus Garvey and Leonard Howell had tried to make it become, before those who didn't care about the Christ purpose of RasTafari took the name and added it to their same old way of life, full of hate and war and indiscipline and bad behaviour, just like the very Babylon that RasTafari was trying to destroy.

But it didn't have that effect. It only gave a lot of people a good reason to exercise their hate on me.

I sighed and once again asked JAH why he always gave me such hard work to do with the writing skills he gave me.

But three months after that article was published, I learned that the miracle I had been praying to JAH for 9 years was finally answered, and I found myself pregnant with my first child, my son Makonnen, at age 44 years.

I took that BLESSING as a sign from JAH that my article was approved by H.I.M.

A MOTHER AT LAST

After the article was published, I went home to my father in Port Antonio. He had retired a few years before I left for England and turned his writing talent and reputation to penning weekly columns in the Daily Gleaner newspaper and writing short books for the JAMAL adult literary programme.

His special opus was *BEAUTIFUL JAMAICA*, a glossy picture book that showcased the best of Jamaica's people, acievements and modern history. It was to become the most famous and popular Jamaican souvenier book, so admired that my father was selected to present a copy to Queen Elizabeth on one of her visits to Jamaica.

Though Pop was glad to see me, his new wife – his fourth -- wasn't. She was a Jamaican country girl from Swift River in the Portland hills, a small community of German-descended, poor-White Jamaicans prized by Jamaican men (and whorehouses) for their skin colour and hair texture.

Only ten years older than me, she hadn't given me a welcome when I came home from England years before, making a quarrel about some kitchenware and plates that my father had given me to set up my Kingston apartment and nagging him constantly until I returned them. It was her second marriage (she had a son from her first marriage, but none with my father) and I stayed away from her as much as I could.

Pop was suffering from unstoppable hiccups and it was an annoying affliction that caused him to have many trips to Kingston doctors in his BMW driven by his wife Vi, short for Viola (I called her 'Virago'). Somehow he seemed to get better whenever his wife drove off to do an errand in Kingston or visit her son at boarding school and we could have some time together, but then the hiccups would return on her return. My poor father! His love for all things White was catching up with a vengeance in his old age!

Hanging out with friends one night on the Titchfield Hill beach facing Navy Island, I met the man who became my husband and baby father.

I had been trying to have a child all during my first relationship after I came home. It had lasted for nine years and as he already had a daughter by a previous relationship, he made me believe our childlessness was because I was barren. I had believed him, but since all that I was learning from the Bible as I was becoming a Rasta told me that all I needed for a miracle to happen was to have faith – even "... as small as a mustard seed", I just started praying, and kept on praying and praying for what became 9 years.

Sometimes I would have a little chat with JAH, you know. "Hey JAH, you said I must have Faith as small as a mustard seed? Well, my Faith bigger than a mustard seed. So I'm still here praying and waiting, you know. Don't forget me plese, JAH. I haven't forgotten YOU!"

So I would chat with JAH every now and then.

For nine years.

Hanging out with friends on the beach at Titchfield Hill, I was asking my friends if any of them knew which stars we were seeing in the clear night sky, when a voice answered from someone further down the beach and a man came over to us and started pointing out various constellations.

I could see this was someone who spent a lot of time in nature, and we introduced ourselves to each other.

"So you are the girl who wrote that article," he said.

I waited for the expected condemnation.

"I liked it. You said the right things."

I was amazed that this brown-skinned, curly-haired Port Antonio man knew about Rasta, and moreover had such a positive view of what I had said. That's when he told me had just cut off his locks after growing them for years, and had even been spending time living with Rastas growing ganja in the St. Ann hills.

He was Deeb Roy Hanna, the 'black sheep' of a Port Antonio family that owned the town's dry goods store, the cinema and several homes in the upper class neighbourhood of Dolphin Bay. Deeb had no such good luck. Illegimate son of one of a family of Syrian Jamaican men with a beautiful St. Elizabeth girl, but her pale skin did not disguise her mother's Black genes and that prohibited her marriage into the Syrian community.

So Deeb grew up the hard way and learned to read only when he was finally 'adopted', aged 11 years, by a

Chinese family who lived in Port Antono, one of whose sons grew up to be Jamaica's yacht-owning billionaire Michel Lee-Chin. Deeb's chance to have a career in his teens as a cruise ship worker was cut short when police arrested him sharing a shore-leave spliff with some Port Antonio friends.

With a police record that would prevent employment for the rest of his life, now he existed as best he could, using his peaceful spirit doing odd jobs around the town, delivering packages, directing the occasional tourists, or helping the market women carry their loads onto and off the country buses.

The Hanna family, doing their best to be seen as the 'White" social and economic leaders of the town, disapproved of Deeb for his association with the Black side of Jamaican life that they were prejudiced against. When the economy of Port Antonio took a nose dive and their businesses began to fail, they failed to see that Deeb was the only family member left with the youth and strength who could help them continue the family business, so one by one they sold the businesses, the buildings and the houses and migrated to America.

Gone were the shops and the many homes. A rich German Baroness turned the cinema into a shopping mall, the dry goods store was taken over by a Jamaican wholesaler, and the spacious family homes became tourist guest houses. No memorial remains today of this once-important Portland family. All either died or moved abroad, except Deeb.

Deeb was a good, upright man living according to Rastafari beliefs and principles, but he was pushed even further from the family for giving the Hanna name to a Black woman. It was said that I had married Deeb 'for money'. When we married I was a Senator who owned my own Lada car and a mortgage on the Ancovy housing scheme 2-bedroom home we lived in. He was homeless, kept his few clothes in a small cardboard box with his Bible, his most precious possession.

But there are so many layers of Jamaican racial and social prejudice.

We bought a Civil License at the Post Office and asked the priest of St. Mary's Anglican Church in Port Antonio, who was our friend, to marry us. We asked the couple living in the apartment beside ours to be the witnesses to our marriage and with just the four of us and the priest, I was married one Tuesday morning.

When the service was over, Deeb sent me to wait for him on the Titchfield Hill beach where we had met and went to the market. He came back with a big fish head given him by one of his market-women friends, a packet of Chicken Noodle soup, some seasoning and an empty cheese can. He built a fire on the beach, boiled the fish head with the Chicken Noodle Soup in the cheese can and we celebrated our wedding feast right there. It was delicious.

Soon after we got married, I was appointed an Independent Opposition Senator. It was a major surprise in my life and a true miracle, coming when it did, so I decided to give thanks by following my young brother Paul's advice to be baptized in the Ethiopian Orthodox Church.

We went into Kingston to celebrate Orthodox Christmas at the January 7 midnight service held at the Holy Trinity Church on Maxfield Avenue. It was a freezing cold night and Deeb advised me not to allow myself to be dipped in the cold water of the little baptismal pool in the Church yard, but I reasoned that if I should die of pneumonia after being baptized, that was OK because my sins had been washed and I was now clean enough to be accepted by my Creator.

The Archbishop dipped my head three times in the water, uttering the benediction and blessing, then gave me my Ethiopian name Makeda and a copy of the Orthodox liturgy.

My Church 'godmother' gave me a white Ethiopian dress to change into, I wrapped my head with a shama and for the rest of the night I was as warm as toast and very happy that I had done something important, something that my beloved Emperor had sent Abuna Yesehaq to do for all of us Rastafari who love H.I.M.

Back in Port Antonio, I took advantage of being a Senator to get a loan to buy an inexpensive Lada car and a license to drive it as a taxi, put on the red Taxi plates, and gave it to Deeb to head out each day to earn our family income by carrying passengers.

I was still praying for a child.

One day I discovered a copy of an Ethiopian Orthodox Prayer of the Virgin Mary that had been 'liberated' from the Magdala Collection in the British Museum by Ras Seymour McLean, a brave RastaMan who felt that the precious prayers that had been stolen from Ethiopia should be returned to Ethiopia and to believers in the faith. The Prayer promises to answer the request of any faithful believer who prays it.

With nothing else to do, I prayed the prayer, which took about an hour to read in its entirety, and I annointed myself as it directed with some holy oil I had received at my baptism at the Orthodox Church in Kingston a few weeks earlier.

One month after I had devoutly prayed the Prayer, I went to see my doctor - the distinguished late Custos of Kingston Dr. John Martin - because my tummy was feeling strange. He made me take some tests, then I returned a few days later to hear the results. To my amazement, I finally found myself pregnant at the age of 44 years. Confirming my pregnancy, Doctor Martin was so surprised that I was pregnant he said in a shocked voice: "It's a miracle, Barbara. Please call one of his names John." (I did.)

My son was born prematurely at 7 months. It was Bob Marley's Birthday February 6 and I had spent the entire day at JBC radio station hosting a call-in marathon to raise funds for Ethiopian famine. I got home at about 10 in the night and my water broke as I lay down to sleep. We were lucky that in the apartment next door lived an older American couple who were Mormons who had just come to live in Jamaica. They had a car and even though they didn't know their way around Kingston, they drove me to the UWI hospital in the night streets.

I was given medication to try and delay his arrival, but my child demanded to be born and came into the world on Saturday evening as the Sabbath was ending.

It was a terrible experience for me. I didn't know if he could live, as there was no water in the womb. But Makonnen insisted on coming into the world. I remember crying out loudly "JAH help us!" as the doctors and nurses surrounded me.

When I finally got to hold his tiny 3 lb. 6 oz. body in the UWI Intensive Care Unit, tears started rolling down my face, but a kind nurse said: "Don't let him see you sad." So instead I sucked back the tears and sang to him one of the hymns I had sung while he was in the womb. *"Praise My Soul, the King of Heaven; to His Feet I tribute Bring."*

When he was in the womb, I would sing my songs of Praise to the Creator for blessing my womb after all these years. Apparently he was listening and hearing. To my great surprise and untold joy, the tiny child stirred in my hands, giving recognition of my voice and presence.

That incident alone made me realize that my child could hear my communication and also communicate with me. I continued talking and singing to him and from that moment on I spoke to him as if he was a grown person, able to understand me perfectly.

His premature birth weight of 3 lbs, 2 oz put his life at risk every day. Two days after he was born Archbishop Yesehaq came to see us to pray over him and annoint him with holy oil. Seeing me in constant tears, he told me to read the First Book of Kings which told the story of Hannah, the barren wife who had prayed for a child in the church.

The Priest Eli had thought she was drunk when he saw her lips moving in his church, but when Hannah told him she was praying for a child, he told her she would have a son and she should raise him in the Church to fulfill the Blessing of her prayers being answered.

The Archbishop's lesson remained for me from that day on, and I resolved that more than anything, I would raise my son to be a faithful follower of the Ethiopian Orthodox way of righteousness.

I also resolved to spell my last name 'Hannah' from that day on. Now I was sure my son was a gift from JAH!

In the three weeks that Makonnen lay in the hospital's Intensive Care Unit, three other babies died, but he survived. The nurses said they called him 'Tiger' because he was such a strong fighter for survival. When it was time to bring the tiny infant home, I was overjoyed and yet frightened.

I had a job at the time organizing the Film Festival of the World Festival of Youth & Sudents being held in Kingston. Then-Minister of Culture Babsy Grange, who met me while we both served as Senators, knew of my experience organizing film festivals and had given me the job and an apartment in Kingston. The plan had been that I would have a Ceasarean birth a few days after the scheduled end of the Festival.

With my baby coming two months earlier than planned, I still had to continue organizing the film festival, so the day after he was born – with stitches underneath and breasts becoming as hard as rocks from milk a baby was waiting for – I packed up my files from the Office of the Prime Minister, took them to the apartment, and with all the drama and emotions of giving birth, I continued working there for two months while nursing a newborn, premature baby.

There were young film makers from many countries who came to the film festival from countries including India, Brazil and Cuba with some good films. But all I remember of the grand Opening Night is that I had to be introducing guests and films on the National Stadium stage, rushing back to the apartment to feed the baby, then rushing back to the Stadium.

It was a tough beginning to a tough life as a mother, but the fact that my nine years of prayers had been answered just months after all the criticism and anger I had received for the "*No more Rasta*" article, was justification to me that what I wrote in it was right in the eyes of JAH.

I was glad to have Archbishop Yesehaq as a blessing in our lives. Within a few weeks he had baptized Makonnen at a very special church service attended by all the Orthodox priests in the Western Hemisphere gathered in Jamaica for a conference.

Abba Yesehaq was to become Makonnen's priestly father, taking a special interest in his life whenever he was in Jamaica and ensuring we both learned how to be good members of the Orthodox faith. His fatherly love and care continued also in America, where we later lived as part of the Church community in New York and New Jersey.

It was a historic time for the Church, as the Mengistu politicians who had overthrown the Emperor and siezed power had removed the Orthodox Patriarch from his post and installed a new Patriarch, contrary to Church tradition which said that a new Patriarch could only be appointed on the death of the previous one. Arcbishop Yesehaq objected strongly to the change and we faithful supported him and made our position known by demonstrating in front of the Ethiopian embassy in New York, where some members were even arrested.

The Archbishop's health never recovered from the battle he fought to protest the unprincipled appointment, and when Jamaican supporters of the new Patriarch insisted on removing the priests ordained by Abba Yesehaq and taking over the church buildings in New York and Jamaica, it changed the Church forever and the Archbishop was never the same.

One last favour I was glad to do for the Archbishop, was to help arrange the first visit to Jamaica of the royal Ethiopian Princes Ermias and Bekere, grandsons of the Emperor and Chairman and Vice-Chair of the Ethiopian Crown Council. The visit was organized by the Church as an

land-wide tour and I used my contacts to arrange first-class
accommodation for the Princes at VIP suites in Round Hill,
Sans Souci, Jamaica Pegasus and Strawberry Hill hotels.

It was wonderful meeting these two Ethiopian royals,
especially Prince Ermias who I feel is such a good example of
his grandfather, that he should be the family member to
inherit the Throne when the Monarchy is restored. When the
visit was ended, the Archbishop and the Princes awarded me
a Gold Adowa Centenary medal on a purple ribbon that is
given to diplomats and royalty. A very high honour indeed.

After the Archbishop died, I found it difficult to return
to the church building and receive communion from those I
felt had betrayed the churchical principles the Archbishop
had stood for. My attendance since then has been sporadic,
usually only for special occasions and only resuming in recent
years when I am usually asked to give a speech at the annual
Memorial Service honouring Archbishop Yesehaq.

But I never stopped raising Makonnen in the
Ethiopian Orthodox faith, as I had promised the Archbishop.

JAMAICA'S MOST UNUSUAL SENATOR

To have been a Senator in the Jamaican Parliament for 4 years was definitely not something I could ever have expected to happen in my life, especially not as a Rasta. It happened at one of the lowest times of my life, but they say when the valley is deep, the mountain top will be high.

I had just come home from England and was living in Port Antonio at my father's house. I had met the man who would become my husband and father to my son, married him and moved with him into a one-room flat on Titchfield Hill. I was trying to survive by writing newspaper articles that paid Two Thousand Dollars when published, and also writing Letters to the Editor expressing my views on anything I felt needed an opinion from an avowed Rastafari member of the nation.

When in 1983 the PNP announced it would not contest the General Election announced by JLP Prime Minister Edward Seaga because the Voters List was incomplete, Seaga went ahead with the election anyway and with no opposition, won all 60 seats in the Lower House, giving Jamaica its first One Party Government.

I wrote two Letters to the Editor on the topic of the Election. In the first I said I agreed with and approved the decision of the PNP not to contest the election, and gave my reasons. Then when Prime Minister Seaga announced that under the circumstances, Parliament would implement the Constitutional clause that permits citizens to address Parliament from the Bar of the House, I wrote a second letter to the Editor saying that I approved of Seaga's announcement to exercise the Constitutional clause and that I intended to exercise this right as a citizen.

With no Opposition, there was now a problem about how to fill the Senate's eight Opposition seats. Consulting the Constitution in which it states that Senators are appointed 'upon recommendation to the Governor General', Prime Minister Seaga recommended to the Governor General eight persons of independent mind who he felt could do the work. I was one of the eight, the only woman and the first Rasta.

I am sure I had come to Mr. Seaga's attention because of my letters. My opinionated views were published often and well known and I am sure he could see that I was not afraid to express them publicly.

But he did not know me. I had never met Mr. Seaga or any members of the JLP until the State Opening of Parliament when we all were sworn in. The 13 faces before me on the Government side at the first sitting of the Senate weeks later, were all new to me with one exception – hotelier John Issa, whose extended family descended from tourism pioneer Abe Issa, had been one of my family friends since my father liberated Issa's Myrtle Bank Hotel swimming pool in a famous anti-racism protest.

Seaga was always portrayed as a terrible person

completely opposite to handsome, charismatic Michael Manley and criticized as a pawn of the USA, whose CIA was later accused of having 'destabilized' Manley's Jamaica. But as both a born-there American-Jamaican and a capitalist, it was no surprise that he was a good friend of the USA and the long list of programmes he introduced and led during his long career as a politician was proof of his fervent nationalism.

The business sector felt Seaga had rescued Jamaica from the deep political and economic pit generated by Manley's closeness to Fidel Castro and Cuba and supported him fervently, but despite all he did he would never be as universaly loved as Manley was.

The nation was divided into two violently opposing political camps and there were few people not aligned to one or the other. Finding himself with a one-Party Parliament, Seaga made a bold decision in his appointment of an Independent Senate, especially of me -- a Rasta and an outspoken member of Jamaica's most controversial group. I was more than glad to accept the invitation to serve as a Senator. It was a very high honour for any Jamaican to have, especially one as controversial and as poor as I was.

But I knew I could do a good job of defending whatever issues came before me and while I was determined not to engage in any kind of confrontational opposition to the Government, I fully intended to express any opposing views I had as diplomatically as possible to maintain a good relationship with all.

Olivia 'Babsy' Grange, who had been mentored by Seaga from her schooldays in Tivoli Gardens and had been as appointed as Senator and Minister of Culture, says Mr. Seaga appointed me "...to represent the people who live simply and take the bus." That was me, for sure!

But my bus days were over, as being in the Senate gave me a chance for a bank loan to buy a car. I bought the cheapest – a brown Russian Lada – to travel to and from Port Antonio for weekly settings of the Senate. Those were the days when Ladas were mostly used as taxis and people were always flagging us down as we drove by, so I licensed the car as a taxi for my husband to drive and help earn our living.

Being a Senator was an intense education in governing. My first, and only, instruction on how to do the job was: "Read the Constitution!" I was given a copy of that very serious document of the laws and practices that control life in Jamaica and I read it thoroughly with eyes wide open.

Second advice was: "Listen and learn!" In this way I sat silently listening for several sittings until I learned how things worked, how speeches were made, the protocols that governed our actions and the powers we had to keep checks and systems of Government in place. We Independent Senators were new to Parliamentary practices, but each of us had some previous association with the political corridors that enabled us to understand the procedures and people that faced us.

The high company I joined in 1984 were Dr. Lloyd Barnett, Q.C., an eminent lawyer who we agreed had the

necessary experience to be our team leader and chief
spokesman; former mayor of Montego Bay Charles Sinclair
who had been both PNP and JLP in his political career; Emil
George Q.C., another eminent attorney; PNP supporters Dr.
Errol Miller, an educator, and Courtney Fletcher, former
President of the Jamaica Agricultural Society; Barbadian
UWI Professor Keith Worrell; and Baptist preacher Rev. C.S.
Reid.

And then there was me. My last job had been as
Director of PR at the Kingston & St. Andrew Corporation, the
mini-Parliament where Councillors of both political sides
defended their turfs and secured benefits for the City of
Kingston communities they represented. The Upper House,
with representatives of Parishes in place of communities, was
no different. I also brought my years of experience in the
Culture division of Michael Manley's Office of the Prime
Minister, where I worked on such projects as CARIFESTA,
the unveiling of the St. Ann statue of Marcus Garvey, the
twinning of Montego Bay with Atlanta, Georgia, and many
more.

Most of all, I was a woman and I was a Rasta – two
groups not yet represented. Mr. Seaga was known as an
expert on all aspects of Jamaican culture, with good reason.
His RASpect of me was bold proof.

To everyone's surprise, the Independent Senate
worked well. The New York Times wrote:

"... *For the first time since Jamaicans were granted
universal suffrage by the British 40 years ago, only one*

political party is sitting in Parliament. To the surprise of almost everyone, this has not stifled debate, but seems to have fostered freer and livelier exchanges than were customary under the traditional two-party system..."

With no political axe to grind, it was not difficult to have good relations with all on both sides. Under the leadership of Ossie Harding as Senate President, the Government Senators were seasoned politicians determined to make their leader's decisions work.

My first independent Debate was a Resolution that Garvey's upcoming 100th Birthday be made a national holiday. After a lively discussion that was even approved by some Government Senators, I and the supporters of my Resolution decided to accept the Government's decision that the holiday would only be for the Parish of St. Ann, Garvey's birthplace. I was content to have made the historic proposal.

As the Senate did not pay a salary, I was happy to accept Senator Grange's offer of a job to arrange a film festival for the World Festival of Youth & Students. With a plan for my baby's birth a week after the film festival ended, I happily worked on the event from a room in the Office of the Prime Minister.

But my son Makonnen came into the world two months early after I had spent a day rushing up and down the stairs of the Jamaica Broadcasting Corporation organizing, at the Prime Minister's request, a radio telethon to raise funds for the Ethiopian famine. My waters broke as I got home that night.

It was a traumatic time as we hoped and prayed that all was well with the small human inside me, but on Bob Marley's birthday he could wait no longer and I became a mother.

I was 44 years old and Makonnen's birth was not how I had planned it. It was hard to deal with the trauma and the stress of giving birth so suddenly and then not even having a baby to take home with me. The baby was kept in the Intensive Care Unit for 3 weeks to to make sure he was alright, then I was able to bring him home and start caring for him myself. It wasn't easy, but my mother became an important help in my life and reassured me constantly.

Thanks to the job, I had been given a small New Kingston studio apartment. The film festival preparation was still happening and there was no way I could get out of doing it. But there was a bright young man, Teddy Laidley, who seemed under-used in the OPM mail room and who was always eager to help whenever I needed. So I recruited Teddy to be my link at the office and continued working on the event from beside Makonnen's crib, notwithstanding stitches underneath and breastfeeding every three hours.

When the festival was over, I returned to Port Antonio with my baby, gratefully accepting a room in my father's home for a few months, while the Minister of Housing Bruce Golding arranged for me to get a small National Housing Trust house on the Anchovy housing scheme that the Government was restoring after a decade of neglect.

Each week Deeb would drive me with the baby over to

Kingston and while they both rested at my brother's house, I would attend Parliament, study the Order Paper and the documents under our review for discussion and endorsement, make my contribution, learn some more about how Government and politics worked, then head back to Portland.

As I said, we Senators on both sides all basically got on well together, with our side carefully scrutinizing all Government proposals and procedures to ensure The People benefited most, and only disputing major issues when we knew they had to be disputed.

For instance, I recall that when Government Senators voted for a postponement of Local Government Elections for a third time, I angrily stated that it was not good enough to deny The People the right to express their opinion so many times, especially considering the fact of the One Party Parliament.

Then I left the Chamber, fed up that I had come to Parliament for no good reason. Cooling down my temper, I made a call to make sure all was OK with my baby being taken care of by his father, then I went back inside to the debate.

Little did I know that my stormy exit was considered a newsworthy action, as reported in the GLEANER the next day that '*Senator Blake-Hanna walked out of the Chamber in tears!*' Gotta smile! Not so, but a good story on which to pin public protest at another election delay.

I can't remember too many details of what we debated

those 30+ years ago. We debated many issues and each Indpendent Senator got to lead a maiden debate on a topic of their choice. I know, however, that all who overheard our presentations say it was 'the best Senate ever'. The New York Times reported in August 1984:

"... *In the Senate this year the Independents have usually voted as a traditional Opposition bloc. But there have been instances of crossover voting by members of both sides. Both Mr. Manley and Mr. Seaga said there had been an increase in effective cricism in Parliament. 'Everyone in Parliament is now acting like the United States,' Mr. Seaga said. "Everyone has his own point of view and they want to speak. They don't have the de facto opposition across from them who will jeer if they make a statement that looks like they're critical of their own party. They get up and they speak their own minds."*

Not all Jamaica was happy with the Independent Senate. Supporters of the PNP were angry, because if we eight individuals had declined the invitation to be Senators, Seaga would have had to call a fresh Election. As a result, many doors were closed to me, especially economic doors, then and for years after. But I survived with pride at having made such an important contribution to the running of the country.

The leaders of the JLP that I met in the Senate went on to become my friends, just as I had become friends with the leaders of the PNP in previous years, and I have remained one of Jamaica's few politically independent individuals. Not tied to either Party, I was free to give my opinion then and I continue to do so today, respected by members on both political sides.

There came a time, though, when the needs of my growing child required a job's salary. The Senate had no salary, as the prestige and honour of being thought good enough to sit in the country's Parliament was supposed to be sufficient pay, so the post was usually given to wealthy members of society. Paying off the car loan and the NHT loan had become impossible, so I resigned the Senate after 4 years to seek income-paying work unencumbered by the title 'Senator'.

There are a few lifelong perks to holding the title 'Former Senator'. One that I love is that any time I wish to visit Parliament to hear a special presentation, I have a very priveleged seat in the Chamber in the row of chairs on the left of the Speaker of the House. I get invited to all special Parliamentary events such as visits by international guests, Joint Sittings and State Openings, and I choose which I attend to get a front-row seat when foreign VIPs address Parliament.

I also gained a first-hand education in how the country is run and how Parliament works, which would be very useful if I ever decide to run for election or make a revolution and take over the country. No such plans yet for either.

Thirty-plus years later, I can look back with pride.

MOTHERING MY SON

After resigning the Senate, I returned to life in Port Antonio and raising Makonnen. I continued teaching him at home, collecting books on all topics and marvelling as he learned to read better and better.

Our Port Antonio house in the new Anchovy Housing scheme was humble. I had received the chance to own the small house by paying a deposit, without having been part of the National Housing Scheme system. There were about 100 houses in the Anchovy community being rebuilt after a decade of empty neglect by the previous administration, but as we were not part of the system, in the beginning we had no electricity or water, just the building.

We had to scrape out rooms full of garbage and install a back door, as the empty house had been used as a goat pen by a nearby farmer, but slowly we managed to find money to install the essential modern features of electricity and running water and make a home for my baby. It wasn't easy as we tried to earn money by operating my Lada as a taxi around Port Antonio.

However, trying to run a taxi did not work out economically to help pay the mortgage on our little house and relations with my husband soured as well, perhaps because of this.

My father died when Makonnen was 3 and it made living in Portland even more sad for me. It was a surprise to me that my father's Will that his widow produced did not mention me. In fact it only left Two Thousand Dollars to the last of my father's six children – a daughter born to a Port Antonio woman – but left absolutely everything to her and her son, so there was no hope of a small financial pillow to rest on. I decided I had to find a job and the only solution was to move to Kingston.

I had met an American woman one day at the Blue Lagoon pool who was doing research for a PhD. thesis on gender relations and who said if I ever came to Kingston I could stay with her. I took her up on her invitation and Professor Suzanne Lafont became one of my best friends for life from thereon.

Staying with Suzanne in Kingston, I went to see Babsy Grange, no longer in Parliament as her Party was no longer in Government, but who was running a PR firm managing reggae artists. I asked her for a job and she readily agreed, but I told her that much as I wanted the work, I was happy with how well my son was learning from my homeschooling, so I didn't want to put him in school. At age 4, Makonnen was already reading well.

"Bring him to the office with you," she said with a smile. "He can stay with you in your office." That was great news. The office was in the modern New Kingston Towers and I found a one-bedroom apartment within walking distance. So I began one of my most interesting and happy jobs ever.

Babsy's company Specs Shang handled reggae artists who she and her partnet Clifton 'Spsecialist' Dillon were making world famous – Shabba Ranks, Yellow Man, Cobra, Patra were some of the artists the company managed and she even gave Damion Junior Gong his first musical bookings as part of a group of children called the Shepherds. There was always at least one reggae artist each day making star-studded entrances to the office and increasing the vibes.

On top of that, the company handled the publicity for Jamaica's first amusement center, Coney Park , where there were rides, games, clowns and fun for people of all ages. I was put in charge of Coney Park's PR, much to the delight of Makonnen who became friends with all the clowns and the girls who gave away prizes at the games booths.

At the same time, next door the office was an agency for educational books run by George Ramocan who became one of Jamaica's High Commissioners to the UK, and his wife Lola, so Makonnen had access to a wonderful library to keep him occupied and to upgrade his knowledge in so many topics.

Makonnen was also learing to use the computer, studying the DOS-based system with black screens and green letters that was how computers operated before Windows was created. He made himself useful by helping when staff wanted to use the new machine they were not accustomed to, typing in the code necessary to log on, helping them find files and create documents.

It was a shame such a good job had to end, but it did, as Babsy moved on to become a full-time politician.

This was a moment when I could have become a GOOD Girl, looked for another Kingston job and put Makonnen in school. I tried enroling him in Mona Prep – a 'good school', where the headmistress was pleasantly surprised to find that he could read well and was brightly intelligent. One problem, though. "You WILL cut his hair, won't you Mrs. Hanna?" she said without smiling. "We don't allow dreadlocks."

No. I had no intention of cutting Makonnen's hair, removing the identification of his priestly dedication I had made at his baptism. I was already set on the Rastafari pathway, with no compromise. I could not consider turning back.

One thing I had noticed while working for the music company was how little trace there was in the music industry of the reggae music Bob Marley had made world famous. The dancehall artists the company represented were the top music stars were from a new genre of Jamaican music called 'dancehall' that didn't have the same beat or vibe as Bob's Rasta reggae music. It seemed like Bob had disappeared just 7 years after his death.

I remembered how vibrant the Seventies had been when Bob and reggae made Jamaica a very interesting place to be. I remembered how wonderful the time had been when

56 Hope Road was the center of the music industry and of Jamaican culture, and of Rasta. I wanted to keep the memory of those times alive.

I put the Anchovy house up for sale, moved out of the New Kingston apartment and took Makonnen with me to Montego Bay, where my brother Paul kept a house ready for whenever Archbishop Yesehaq went there to minister to the MoBay Church. Paul gave us a bedroom there.

I had started writing my novel '*Joseph – a Rasta Reggae Fable*' by candlelight at nights in the Anchovy house after Makonnen fell asleep, so I decided to live off the money left from the house sale after paying off the mortgate, and finish writing the book I hoped would become a best-seller and earn me money for life.

The Montego Bay house was in the hills outside the town and a good place to write a book. Every few days we would go into the town and spend the day at the public beach, treat ourselves to lunch at a small Chinese restaurant, and then head back up the hill. The money lasted for several months of life in Montego Bay and I finally finished writing the book.

When the money finished, I was satisfied I had accomplished my objective. I now had my first novel. All I needed was a publisher.

I also needed to find somewhere else to live. My brother Paul stopped renting the MoBay house, as the Archbishop moved his headqarters to New York and Paul went to live in Philadelphia. There are not many options for

Rastas to find employment or housing and from Makonnen's birth I had started growing my locks to keep him company. No one would employ me with dreadlocks , as those were not the days when dreads were the fashion hairstyle worn by trendy ladies today. Moreover, being a 'former Senator' was more of a disadvantage in those PNP years, than an asset.

Before he left Jamaica, the Archbishop told me there was a place in Kingston where members of the Orthodox Church lived, especially the priests-in-training, and suggested we could live there. I took his advice. and blessing, and moved with Makonnen to Debre Zeit – a small capture-land community of simple houses on the mountainside of the Hope River by the road going up to Gordon Town above Kingston.

Big Daddy, a big Rastaman who was 'father' of the community, gave us a small old house made of wattle and daub with a thatched roof, in which I put our few bits and pieces. We had a tent I had bought to camp out at Reggae Sunsplash one year, and I pitched it on the land beside the house, put the carpet I bought in Iraq on the ground with our blankets as a bed, preferring to sleep there because the old house had insects of all kinds living in the thatch.

Brother Zaddik, a fiery Orthodox Rastaman, lived close by and was known to be fierce enough to be both a protector and caretaker to us both. He became another father figure to Makonnen, teaching him the secrets of country life, plants and animals. With him and Big Daddy around, we had no fear of living at Debre Zeit and soon got to know the other Church people and children living there.

I had to cross the river two times to get home or out again, stepping on stones, or taking off my shoes when necessary, using a strong stick to support me as I carried little Makonnen by my hand. When the river was full. one of the comunity's strong men would put Makonnen on his shoulders and take us across, while I would follow fearfully behind, holding my breath and praying that he would not slip and fall in.

But apart from that danger, it was heaven living by the river and Makonnen and the community children had fun in it every day, swimming, fishing, exporing the countryside and enjoying being free in nature. He grew to know the hillside well, once leading a film crew up the river to the waterfall at a rapid pace for a little 7-year-old boy, that impressed them so much they paid him a nice fee.

It was a simple life, nothing like I had ever before experienced, but I was proud to be living in nature according to my Rastafari principles and keeping Makonnen smiling and happy. Those were the only two things that mattered to me.

I would earn little bits of money writing articles on my portable typewriter and taking them to the Daily Gleaner for publication in a weekly column, or as feature articles. Little Makonnen made friends with the staff he met on these occasions, who found him unusual and bright. One would give him copies of '*Popular Mechanics*' magazines that taught him so much, and another would give him '*Archie*' comics that made him laugh. The canteen had good cheap lunches that would fill our bellies for the day. We lived simply.

Sometimes friends would put a small assignment my way that earned me a few more Dollars, and these were the ways I supplied Makonnen and myself with life's basics.

Sad to say, neither Big Daddy nor Brother Zaddik are still with us. One day a lady living close to Brother Zaddik's little house was alerted by a bad odour and found that he had died a few days earlier. I was so sad that I had not known how little food he was eating or how few resources he had to feed himself. He didn't deserve to die that way.

Big Daddy also operated a fruit stall on the main road to Gordon Town, just before the turn-off we would take to begin crossing the river to Debre Zeit. It was our little market. One day he disappeared and we have never heard anything about him since. It is suspected that he was killed by some of the badmen who he worked hard to keep from using the hills around Debre Zeit as their hiding place. His body was never found.

What makes his disappearance more sad, is that he had only recently found a woman who gave him his first child, a girl, and he was overjoyed to have finally become a father. He is missed by all who knew him and we still think of him when we drive past the fruit stall that is now being run by his baby-mother and growing daughter.

Angels don't stay long on Earth. They do their angelic work and return to Zion to keep Our Father company.

THE HOMESCHOOLING YEARS

My second published book was *"Home The First School: A Homeschooling Guide to Early Childhood Education"*. I wrote it when Makonnen was 13 years old and had just made world news by being appointed the Youth Technology Consultant to the Goverment. That appointment finally answered all those who had criticised my choice to homeschool my son, told me I was mad and that he 'would never amount to anything'.

The book tells how and why it happened, and the story is long enough to deserve covers of its own. However, let me share some of the early words that explain WHY I did it and HOW.

First of all, the HOW is that I gave my child a lot of LOVE. I loved my child so much, I just wanted to give him as much Love as it was possible for a human to give and to receive. I was so grateful for his presence on earth and in my arms and I gave JAH Thanks every day for giving me that little baby to give all my Love to. I didn't want him to ever be in the hands of anyone who did not love him as much as I did and I knew that because of how he looked to different from most other children, not everyone would want to show him love.

WHY I did it was because, as a Rasta, I wanted him to have a different package of information on which to build his thoughts, knowledge and actions than the information he would receive from traditional education. I wanted him to grow as a Rasta too, with RASpect for the history of his race and culture and people and spirit. I especially didn't want him exposed to the 'White Jesus' type of 'Christian' information taught in schools, that I had already rejected

I set very high standards for the information I wanted him to be exposed to and I wanted to make sure that he would have as wide a foundation of all kinds of knowledge as early as possible, that I knew he would not receive from an education like the one I had received in the Anglo-Jamaican system.

On this foundation, I set certain goals to ensure I would achieve my objective. For instance, as a priority I tried to make sure that he never cried, and when he did, I was quick to solve whatever problem caused the upset. I hate to hear a child cry, worst of all my own child. It hurts my heart. I believed he did not deserve whatever was causing his distress and I hastened to find the solution that would return him to his happy state of innocence.

I breastfed him. I had promised myself that I would let my child breastfeed as long as he wanted, because – I reasoned – breast milk was his food that he had brought with him into the world. How could I deprive him of the nourishment that his existence had caused my body to make?

I would do nothing to stop him from consuming the nourishment he had brought with him into the world.

I had read two important bits of information, the first that breast milk contains nourishment for brain development that cannot be duplicated in man-made milk. This led me to assume that baby food made from cows milk or other animals would promote development of intelligence only as great as that of the animal.

The second piece of useful information was the advice from the La Leche League (Leche is French for 'milk') an excellent, US based organization that encourages mothers to breastfeed. One way, La Leche advises, to overcome the shame and social stigma of the exposed breast, is to wear two-piece outfits with blouses that can be lifted up for baby's access, then dropped over for modesty. La Leche also advised that a light scarf worn around the mother's neck can also be used for extra cover.

As a Rastawoman, I easily adapted to these practices and noted that my child fed and slept even better with his little covering. I could breastfeed anywhere – on the bus, in an office, among people or alone. No one could penetrate our privacy.

I noticed that whatever I read to him or said to him while he was breastfeeding, seemed to stick in his brain. One day when he was 7 months old, I was reading again his "ABC" book that featured "C" for 'chair' beside a picture of a green-backed chair with a woven straw seat. My son abruptly got off the breast, crawled out of my lap, across the floor and stopped beside a brown wooden chair with plaid fabric seat.

The expression on his face asked: "Is this a chair?" So I said "Yes, that is a chair."

He returned to my lap with a look of satisfaction, and we continued reading. My view through this moment into his learning mind, caused me to concentrate even more deeply on the information I was pouring into his brain. I started pasting up pictures on the wall of our small living room which eventually became his 'school room' for 4 years. I put up photos of the animals that were only drawings in his storybooks – bears, lions, horses, whales. I put up a Map of the World, pictures of the Planets and Constellations, replicas of Ancient Egypt and African art.

We spent hours looking through the pictures in a large recipe book, that showed him the existence of such foods as strawberries, soufflés and stroganoff. On walks, we collected leaves from the different trees and plants we passed and learned to recognize their differences, then took them home for our collection. I made him realize that everything in Creation had a name, and we could learn them all. Learning them meant speaking their names, then writing them, so his vocabulary grew with his knowledge.

As his vocabulary grew, I saw there were certain things he was very interested in. He loved 'building' his toys into piles, so I visited the local lumber yard and collected a box of wood scraps and ends of all shapes. This box of simple building blocks became his most favourite toy ever, replaced only when an angel from California named Sumati Bellesly brought him his first Lego set just before his second birthday.

The ability to create things out of his own mind, was important to develop his confidence and give him power over his own thoughts.

But favourite above all were his toy cars, and he had a big collection of little Matchstick cars that were minatures of all the popular models. The first place he could identify on our wall Atlas was Taiwan, as most of these miniatures bore the trademark "Made in Taiwan".

In the early years when I was a Senator, we traveled on the road a lot from our Port Antonio home to Kingston, and to while away the journey we would call out the names of the big vehicles we passed. Most of all he loved Leyland trucks, and shouted with glee each time one of the monsters approached us on the road. He soon asked to be called "Big Truck" and introduced himself as such when asked his name.

One day when he was a little more than 2, we were driving back home to Portland from my weekly trip to the Senate in Kingston, when my son pointed to a car on the road and said "Mummy, that's a Porsche."

I was totally flabbergasted! I didn't know that he even knew what a Porsche was, let alone able to recognize it on the road aged 2. When I asked him how he knew it was a Porsche, he said it was because he had a minature that was made in Taiwan.

As the journey continued, I considered that if he could recognize a Porsche, and recognize it as different from a Leyland truck, he could recognize a letter.

So was born the Alphabet Wall, which I recommend to every parent. I set aside a section of our living room wall and divided it into 26 sections. Then I pasted up a red card with the letters "T" and "t", plus a picture of a truck. Within a week, he could recognize the letter T anywhere – in books, on road signs, and even make a T with his blocks.

The next week I put up the letters "M" and "D" for Mummy and Daddy. After a week, M and D were added to his knowledge. The next week I put the letter "P" for Porsche, then "L" for Leyland. We continued at random in this way, not starting at A, as is usually done, but by the names of his favourite things.

I taught him the letters at random because I noticed that when the friends who came to play with him – children even as old as 10 -- recited the ABC, they got lost when they got to the sounds "L-M-N-O-P", which they pronounced as "ellem–en-o-pee". For them the Alphabet was just a series of sounds they recited as best they could, without knowing what they were referring to.

But in less than 20 weeks, my son could recognize the entire Alphabet and could tell me where any letter came in the alphabet, by remembering its place on his Alphabet Wall.After being able to recognize letters, it was easy for him to learn to recognize small words.

In a book I learned that there are only 2,000 of the most-used words in the English language, and that most of them are simple words such as "the, it, and, up, to, he, she, go, come," and so on. Word recognition became my method of teaching him to read, because English has no consistent pronunciation of co-joined letters; the Phonics of English do not follow as standard a path as – say – Spanish.

For example: why are the letters 'ea' in "lean" and "learn" pronounced differently? Would it be correct to spell "fish" as 'ghoti" if we use the "f' sound of "gh" in 'tough' and the 'sh' sound of 'tio' in "motion"?

I didn't start out to teach my son an entire school curriculum, only to give him some basic lessons as a starter. I wanted to give him a foundation of knowledge that he could build on successfully, despite the limitations I saw in the school system. I believe that Education is really about life and the tools we need to live life abundantly. A child needs core values on which to build its life. However, as our educating continued, I realized I was giving him an enriched version, better than he could obtain in a classroom with other infants vying for the attention of a single caretaker 'teacher'.

Living in the country gave me many teaching opportunities, especially about nature. To show a child the beauty of a flower and explain its composite parts; to walk with a herd of goats and talk about the life of animals; to look for shells along a seashore or to sit quietly and watch the sun go down over far away hills, all gave many chances for me to embed some important values in my child which I feel are the fundamentals of all 'education'.

Finding a dying bird was a chance to talk about life and death and nature and God's purpose. Watching a caterpillar grow into a chrysalis and then a butterfly, taught the wonders of nature, biology and science. Helping a baby chicken get back into its mother's nest taught mercy and kindness. These are the 'values and attitudes' we must pour into a child. The countryside gave me many teaching opportunities.

I found we could use ten of the shells we collected at the beach, to make the sounds 1-10 while dropping them into an empty margarine tub. The noise delighted him, both of the shells and my counting. Soon he began to imitate my actions and sounds. In these informal ways began our Maths curriculum.

Seeing results encouraged me still further and I followed my heart while dredging my brain of all the learning it possessed, investigating how it came there, and thinking about ways to download it to this new brain. I still thought I would soon have to send him to 'school', but I was glad to have the time I saw was necessary to give him as much preparation and foundation as I could.

When he started reading at the age of 2, I saw that my work was bearing fruit and that I was giving him a valuable tool that the majority of Jamaican children did not have, so I was determined to continue as long as I could. Makonnen's ability to read meant that he could learn anything he wanted to know from books, and they became his favourite toy.

Makonnen's library included storybooks from countries like China, Africa, Egypt and Brazil, Greek and Roman mythology, astrology, science and cuisine. He knew about planets, dinosaurs, whales and gnocci. He could build a car following the instructions on the Lego box and then build one himself using the parts and pieces of other boxes.

When I started working on a DOS computer, he learnt the codes for various tasks and whenever the computer crashed (as computers did in the early days), he would watch keenly as the repair man typed the codes for various tasks.This basic DOS information stayed with him and formed the basis for his in-depth knowledge of computers.

Today, there is almost no computer programme or function that he does not understand. His un-schooled knowledge continually amazes me because he has never had lessons in computer technology, but it should be expected because thanks to being homeschooled, since childhood from the very beginning of personal computers he has had the opportunity and leisure to investigate every single aspect of computers as his curiosity inspires him.

Everyone was always surprised at how much Makonnen knew about computers and technology in those years when computers were rare things that few people had and the internet had just started. But Makonnen had been using a computer from the time when computers had black screens with green writing and DOS was the system of code that had to be used to access the programmes and websites built using HTML code.

He grew up when Windows first started, becoming one of the original 'techies' and the first one in Jamaica to come to internationao attention. When Bill Gates heard of Makonnen's appointment as Youth Technology Consultant to the Minister of Technology, he sent the Minister two tickets to come and see him. Minister Paulwell didn't take Makonnen with him, taking instead a Ministry official, Peter King, (whose murder a few years later became one of Jamaica's biggest scandals!)

When we asked the Minister afterwards about Bill Gates, he reported it was a 'disappointing' meeting. I think Bill Gates was surely disappointed that the Minister did not bring his dreadlocksed techie to meet him!

People who remember Makonnen's history-making appointment wonder why he did not go on to become a 'Jamaican Bill Gates'. We certainly tried to get the Minister's promise fulfilled to set up our annual summer TechSchool Jamaica into a permanent learning space for Jamaican tech teens and if that had happened, he would certainly have used his technology knowledge to go on to greater heights and income.

But after waiting a few years and other lost opportunities for this to happen, Makonnen turned his attention to his first interest and skills in music, just at the precise moment when music studio production changed and became upgraded from analog to digital. This caused a host of new technology programmes to be created to record and make music, giving birth to a new musical era.

It was here that Makonnen's superior tech knowledge provided an appropriate outlet for his creative energies and he has been producing and recording music by computer ever since with great success, having two of his songs on two Grammy-nominated albums so far and working towards his own Grammy.

Making music is what he has done with his early and personally acquired knowledge of the emerging technology that is now global. For a moment in time, Makonnen was the most famous young person in the world, written about in major international publications, speaking at M.I.T., the UN and Harvard.

It is a life achievement worth remembering forever.

TRAVELS WITH MAKONNEN

The job with the Minister of Technology had come about as a result of a visit we made to the Minister Phillip Paulwell to ask him for support of the first TechSchool Jamaica, a summer school Makonnen and I held in a room at the Mona Heights house where we lived and which my brother Peter operated as a music studio. We had invited 8 of the techies Makonnen had been working and playing with online, and as teachers we invited some adults from Microsoft and Fujitsu, as well as Computer Paul who was working at the studio with the first digital music programmes, to share their knowledge.

While in the Minister's office Makonnen noticed a box with computer equipment sitting in a corner and asked the Minister about it. He replied that he was waiting for someone to come and set it up on his desk, as he knew nothing about computers. With his permission, Makonnen opened the box and set up the Minister's computer in the twinkling of an eye.

The Minister was so impressed at the high level of tech knowledge Makonnen had, that right on the spot he invited Makonnen to become his Consultant to inform him about what was going on in the world of technology, which children had become so adept at using.

Minister Paulwell readily agreed to give Ministry

support and some funding to the first TechSchool and used Makonnen to advise him on what youths were doing with computers, as they seemed to know best how to use this new device that was changing the world.

Makonnen's appointment made world news. It was an overwhelming experience to be in the spotlight, being interviewed by international news media from the leading newspapers, radio and TV in America, Britain, France, Germany and Japan, the most famous of which were the BBC, TIME Magazine, the Los Angeles Times, Newsweek, tech magazine Wired, and the Miami Herald.

The LA Times sent a reporter who spent three days with us, and whose article filled the front and back pages of the presitious newspaper's weekend Entertainment edition, with a photo of Makonnen on the front page and his story continuing on the back page around a photo of the famous actress Shirley McLaine.

'National Geographic for Kids' did a major colour feature on Makonnen, accompanied by a photo of him enjoying the beach with some of the young surfing Wilmot children, to go with the headline "*Jamaican Tech Teen Surfs the Internet*". TIME for Kids gave him a cover headline and story inside their children's edition.

There was no salary for the job, as Makonnen was under the legal age of employment, so he received only a monthly honorarium. But part of the deal was a promise to set up the TechSchool summer project into a real school, where Makonnen could help train the bright Jamaican techies like him to take a serious step into the world of technology and its use in education.

Makonnen's appointment opened many interesting doors to new countries and people. But best of all were his international invitations. Within days of the news breaking, we received an invitation from the Massachusetts Institute of Technology (MIT) to join an internet forum they had set up inviting children around the world to participate in an online dialogue about a variety of topics. Makonnen chose education, focusing on using computers and the internet.

From the thousands who participated, Makonnen was one of the one hundred children of all nationalities and cultures invited to Massachusetts for Junior Summit – a week of interacting with the brightest minds at MIT and the brightest young minds who had entered the new world of digital technology.

It was wonderful to be inside MIT, seeing the amazing tech inventions they were working on and meeting some of the most brilliant teachers and tech minds of that great institution. One special session was at the Lego Institute headed by the great educator Prof. Seymour Paepert, who first explained the connection between building Lego and using computers in education and who spent most of his career teaching and researching at MIT. Lego introduced its Mindstorms robotics programme, at Junior Summit. My Lego-fanatic son was quite at home here.

Another trip was to Harvard, where Professor Charles Nesson who had read about Makonnen's appointment in the

New York Times, had made a special trip to Jamaica to meet him and invite him to the University, saying he would arrange for him to receive a scholarship to enter pre-university and later Harvard itself.

It was an amazing offer, but I had to think deep about handing over my sheltered and inexperienced 14-year Rasta youth to live with a strange American couple in an unknown situation in a foreign country. Perhaps if the offer had included a job for me where he would have someone he knew close at hand, Makonnen would probably now be a Harvard graduate – living a new life as one of the Green Card-owning Jamaicans who disappear into the American world and live their most important lives away from home.

But for Makonnen, with his optimism not yet soured by politicians' promises, he preferred to stay in Jamaica and wait for his dream of heading a technology training school for Jamaican students to become reality. Makonnen said that he could learn all he wanted to know in Jamaica, especially about the music he loved, and he definitely did not want to be separated from the person he had spent his life with and on whose love and guidance he still depended as a child.

So we turned down that invitation. Instead Makonnen visited Harvard a year later to spend a summer teaching music production at a Harvard summer school and can now put 'University Lecturer' on his Bio.

The Professor remained our friend for years after and both Makonnen and I have worked with him since then on several projects he has initiated in Jamaica. One was the setting up of the first computer labs for inmates in the Gun Court and the General Penitentary prisons. I remember the concert the GP inmates presented at our first visit, with little Makonnen wide-eyed to see what life was like inside the General Penitentary, and where one of the star performers in the show was 'Leppo', the man who killed Peter Tosh!

But sad to say, the promise of our TechSchool was never kept.

Our next foreign trip was to Hollywood, California – yes, the real movie city. When Mak's tech job was announced, we were contacted by two American homeschooled teenagers (and their parents) inviting us to join them as members of a team building a website in the ThinkQuest international student website competition. ThinkQuest invited students to work online with their teachers to build an interactive website on a subject of choice to win prizes of scholarship funding, and a trip to Hollywood.

Melissa Sconyers and her boyfriend Jory Hanus lived in Austin, Texas with their parents and both had been home-schooled from birth, like Makonnen. They read about him in their hometown newspaper and invited him to work with them on a website they were building called 'eBiz4Teenz', teaching teens how to become entrepreneurs. The website was built entirely by digital communication online between Makonnen, Melissa and Jory.

Those were the early days of the internet and as international phone calls were beyond my Jamaican pocket, it was good to communicate this way. As they all were homeschooled, their mothers and I as their teachers were part of the team, providing supervision and support as they worked.

Melissa was later named 'the US Top Tech Teen', so you can see what minds united to build the website. Thankfully after all that work between Jamaica and Texas, their project was selected for the Finals and the three teenagers, along with us three mothers/teachers were flown to Hollywood, California for an Awards weekend hosted by the city's Mayor.

It was a wonderful way to see Los Angeles and Hollywood with Makonnen. Among the visit's highlights was a ride along Bob Marley Boulevard in Universal Studios theme park, seeing sets where many famous movies had been made with artificial floods, moving scenery and a 'Back To the Future' ride among the attractions. Later we were treated to a fabulous dinner in one of the huge film sound stages, where actors dressed as well-known Hollywood stars circulated among the tables entertaining us. Marilyn Monroe's stop beside the dreadlocksed Makonnen was the subject of many photographers flashbulbs!

The 'eBiz4Teenz' website won 2nd prize in the Interdisciplinary section and we all, students and teachers, received awards and cash. Before leaving Los Angeles, Melissa and her mother invited Makonnen and me to visit them in Austin, Texas and flew us to spend a lovely week with them in their lovely home in the lovely city.

Melissa and Makonnen met up again a few months

later when the NASA Kennedy Space Center invited them to join three other top US techies for the launch of the Space Center's Conference Center in Orlando, Florida.

It was a wonderful opportunity to be right there in the heart of the US space programme, standing beside huge towering space ships, touring the museum to see space suits, capsules that had been to the Moon and back, and videos of astronauts telling stories of their trips. Makonnen made the most news as the only non-American given such a noteworthy invitation.

We travelled the Caribbean also. The Trinidad & Tobago Chamber of Commerce invited Makonnen to address students on a visit with the Minister, and delighted them when he told the teacher who asked about the danger of students watching pornography if they were allowed to have internet access, that porn takes too much time to download, as opposed to video games that they much preferred. Minister Paulwell was proud of him and proud of his decision to appoint Makonnen that had made him the most interesting of the world's new technology politicians.

We made a second trip to Trinidad when Optimists International invited Makonnen to be a speaker at their Caribbean Convention. He had impressed them when he spoke at their Kingston gathering and he considered him a good example for their focus on youth. He was the star speaker at that event and we had another good time in Trinidad.

The most interesting Caribbean trip of all was to

Guyana, where we had a variety of experiences that showed the diversity of that vast South American nation. Invited through a Jamaican woman who headed the Jimmy Carter Foundation's Caribbean operations, Makonnen had an assignment to meet with and inspire Guyanese students all over the country.

First we visited a school in downtown Georgetown in a historic old wooden building with Black students who seemed like Jamaican 'downtown' children.

To get to another school, we were taken by ferry across a huge river then by road to a modern, well-equipped school recently opened by Britain's Prince Charles that was populated almost entirely by Indian-race students. The contrast between the schools for Blacks and Indians said a lot about Guyana.

There were other sides to Guyana that we got to see. One evening in Georgetown we got a chance to meet the Rastafari community there and talk with them about topics like education (they were impressed that Makonnen was being home-schooled) and how important was technology in education from a Rastafari perspective. I was pleased to see the Guyana Rastafari people, as they were to see us.

Another special trip was by small plane to Linden, a town deep in the interior of Guyana right on the border with Brazil. I had to hold my breath as the small plane flew over 'the largest gold mine in the world' – a deep slash into the earth far below in the middle of the Guyana jungle – before landing at a small village in Amerindian country of cattle farms spreading over large savannas.

There, the population was mostly Amerindian, a people I had never met before. The Mayor of the town was a woman who gave us breakfast, offering iguana and snake – if we wished – with pancakes and syrup, then took us for a walk through cashew trees in which lived huge, bright green iguanas. Thank heavens I am not afraid of lizards, or I couldn't live in Guyana!

At the school of Amerindian children I saw among the children the most beautiful girl I had ever seen, an Amerindian with brown eyes, brown skin and long dark brown hair. We are still friends and she is even more beautiful today. The innocence in all their faces showed they lived quiet lives according to a cultural tradition different from the rest of the country's African and East Indian people.

Later, as the village celebrated Guyana Independence with a small concert at the local town hall, the young girl and her schoolmates danced a Rodeo Dance, showing the community's reliance on cattle farming, a very different way of life and culture.

Before we left Guyana, Makonnen gave a main speech to the public at a Georgetown hotel, after which he was praised by the daughter of Guyana's former Premier Forbes-Burnham, who attended. Everywhere we went, Makonnen was treated like a very special VIP and everyone was impressed by the 15-year old who knew computers so well that the Government had employed him.

The most important trip Makonnen made, however,

was his first visit to speak at the United Nations in New York. The first, yes, because he impressed the United Nations so much that he was invited to return 3 months later and speak again in an even higher forum. The Tech Ministry was participating in an early initiative to unite the Caribbean countries in a Caribbean Youth Digital Diaspora and Makonnen was invited to give a speech.

Flown to the USA by the UN, I had just renewed my UK passport and didn't carry the old one with me that had my US Visa, that I had been forced to get after overstaying one of my visits to New York. So Immigration refused to let us into the USA and held us both overnight at the airport in preparation to sending us back home, despite my explanation that we were guests of the United Nations and my pleas for overstanding.

All they offered was to allow Makonnen in on his own, as his British passport did not need a Visa, but when I refused indignantly, I realised the offer was just a test to see if I was trying to get him to illegally enter the USA.

I spent a sleepless night sitting up on a hard bench in the room where people waiting to be deported were held, while Makonnen got a little rest on my shoulder. It wasn't easy hearing behind me the sobs of a woman who had tried to get into the US with false papers and knew she would be returned after spending hard earned money and desperate hopes. I gave her a word of comfort, but not too much as I didn't want it to look like I knew her and was part of her attempt.

Fortunately, by morning the Immigration officers had looked us both up on the internet and seen confirmation of the UN invitation, so at 6 a.m we were told we could enter the US. It took a while to get from the airport and with no opportunity change or even eat food, we rushed to the UN and found the luncheon where the launch was taking place. It had just started, so almost breathless Makonnen plugged in his laptop, started the PowerPoint slides and gave his speech.

He was an absolute sensation, the young man with dreadlocks speaking like he knew everything about technology. In a bright moment in a long programme of boring speeches by Caribbean government officials, Mak's tech star shone brightly.

We had hardly returned home when a letter came from the UN inviting Makonnen to speak again at a forum three months later in the Economic & Social Council (ECOSOC) – the second highest Assembly at the UN, in a programme that was being chaired by the Jordanian Queen Mother. Most of the speakers were from international organizations that were using technology in various ways, such as in hospitals, factories and data-gathering and they were all very boring.

I could see everyone losing interest, as the afternoon wore on drearily with one boring speech after another. Five o'clock was approaching, people were gathering their papers and some were leaving when Makonnen went to the podium and opened his laptop. From the computer came the sound of Bob Marley and reggae. Everyone stopped in their tracks, as the youth with dreadlocks told them about how technology was the key instrument in Jamaica's growing digital music industry. He received a resounding applause.

At the reception that followed, Makonnen was the undoubted star to whom all the delegates wanted to speak. I remember a photo of him standing between two diplomats – one from Africa and one from Lebanon – nationalities united by a young Rasta boy. Both Makonnen and I felt a sense of relief at this bright moment in his and our lives.

Makonnen's computer-based education will become the norm globally. It is good to have been a pioneer.

MAKONNEN THE MOVIE STAR!

We have travelled outside Jamaica on other occasions afterwards, especially when dreams were not materialising and it seemed possible there were economic opportunities outside Jamaica.

Once we stayed in New Jersey, thanks to my brother Paul who was a very faithful disciple of the Ethiopian Orthodox Church and humble assistant to our beloved Archbishop Yesehaq who lived there as priest of the Bronx EOTC church. Paul found us a place to stay in the Church building that had accommodation upstairs for the clergy, including the Archbishop, and we invested in two air tickets to New York.

Everyone loved Makonnen and knew him because he had been baptized after his birth by the Archbishop at a service in Kingston attended by all the priests of the EOTC in the West, most of whose churches had been established by the Archbishop. He called Makonnen his 'godson' and because of the Archbishop, we were well received by members of the Church, especially by the Rutty family.

We stayed in the Bronx church house for a while until the Rutty family invited us to live with them in New Jersey. Mikel Rutty and his wife Askale had 6 children and were faithful Orthodox Rastafari. Their house could barely hold them, but their beautiful hearts opened to welcome a mother and her child trying to find a source of income and survival in America. Makonnen loved living with the four Rutty boys who were all nearly his age and life in New Jersey was a good base for us to see another side of life.

New York itself was another good education for Makonnen. We got to know the city by many trips around its various interest spots. We visited the famous F.A.O. Schwartz toy shop opposite the Plaza Hotel and saw the big piano Tom Hanks played with his feet in the movie 'Big". I personally enjoyed going inside the famous New York Library to see its vast collection, and I took Makonnen to Harlem and showed him the Schomberg Museum where I had researched Garvey for my Rastafari book. One favourite trip was to eat in the inexpensive backstreet Chinatown restaurants.

My good friend Suzanne LaFont who had given me a way out of Port Antonio, had by this time earned her PhD. from Yale and was now a Professor, living in a flat in uptown Manhattan close beside Central Park and often invited us to stay over with her. She gave us many lovely experiences of New York life, especially introducing us to the wonders of the Natural History Museum where Makonnen and I spent many happy hours marveling at its many collections.

Among our many good memories was spending Thanksgiving Day with Suzanne and her family watching the grand floats and colourfully costumed groups that gathered in the street at her block before the start of the Macy's Thanksgiving Day Parade, then enjoying Thanksgiving dinner with her husband Anders and son Eric.

Suzanne again arranged for me to lecture to her undergraduate class at Kingsborough Community College. But ultimately, my hope that I could live in America on income from selling my books, lecturing or from writing, did not materialize.

I had written a review of the newly-published and controversial *"The Book of Jamaica"* the prestigious 'Village Voice' paper was about to publish, but I withdrew it when I realized that something I wrote in it would offend top people in Jamaica, even if it was an honest statement.

Publication in that paper would have ensured my recognition as a journalist by the top NY publications, but I eventually realized it was best to return to Jamaica and try again to live there successfully while maintaining the principles and thinking I now held as a Rastafari woman. New York was not for me. Two blizzards in a row that covered the streets with hugh snowdrifts, helped make up my mind.

Another sweet stay in the USA was several years later, when we were invited to bring a film we had made *"Kids Paradise – The Great Lost Treasure Hunt*' to the Chicago Childrens' Film Festival. The film was based on a story Makonnen suggested I should write about a group of children who find a 'treasure map' while staying at a North Coast hotel, and their adventure on beach and boat that takes them to a sweet conclusion.

Reggae star Freddie McGregor played the lead adult

male, and beautiful Gina Jarrett played Makonnen's aunt, while her daughter Sky was one of the children and leading singer Karen Smith did a cameo performance.

Flown to Chicago by the Festival organizers, we stayed first in a hotel and enjoyed the festival week, where we were treated like celebrities. Makonnen was hailed as a 'Jamaican Peter Pan' and our film won an Audience Approval award.

I had two sets of friends in Chicago, one a Jamaican we had met years before and the other a White family we had met in Negril who invited us to stay with them after the film was shown.

Our White friends, a cancer surgeon and his at-home wife, lived with their two daughter in the posh Oak Lawn suburb of Chicago where great architect Frank Lloyd Wright had set the high building aesthetic. The neighbourhood had elegant two- and three-storey homes set back from the road with broad, unfenced lawns and people rode bicycles to the nearby posh shops. It was good to see America from this space.

We visited the Shedd Aquarium with its amazing collection of sea creatures of all kinds, the Navy Pier with its patio of spurting fountains, and a posh school with a pool that had a shoreline entry that made it look like a beach.

Our Black friends in Chicago, on the other hand, were Jamaican-Americans who invited us to stay with them in the Black Chicago neighbourhood of Southside. The residents were mostly Black Americans, with some Mexicans. It was interesting spending time there among two cultures, African and Latino -- seeing the difference of Black supermarkets full of frozen turkey, packaged pork and collard greens on one side and more prosperous-looking Mexican-American shops on the other side of the neighbourhood selling food I recognized as a Jamaican like green bananas, ripe plantain, avocado and chocho.

Staying on the Black side gave the opportunity to introduce my Chicago Rastafari friends to the Ethiopian Orthodox Church, making a visit to a nearby church on two occasions and teaching them some rituals and traditions.

I was also using the Chicago trip to link with a Chicago-based Rastafari publishing company with which I was negotiating to publish a new edition of *"Rastafari – The New Creation"*. I had sent them a digital copy of the book and all its illustrations, and was expecting that the book would be published and I would have copies to take back to Jamaica before the 3 months allowed in my Visa expired.

Not only did I overstay my time as I waited and begged and pleaded with the publisher to fulfill his agreement, but my ticket expired and it took me weeks before I managed to get the money to get us out of America that time. Thankfully, JAH sent a lion to care for us while we waited and Makonnen will never forget all he learned from that strong lion.

The publisher never gave me any books. From time to time I would see one or other of the other pictures I sent him appearing in other books they published. I never got an apology or an explanation. A friend said that perhaps I hadn't paid enough, not just money. There's always a price too high for me to pay.

BECOMING A UNIVERSITY LECTURER

My first invitation to speak at a University had come many years earlier, when my great American girlfriend Prof. Suzanne LaFont invited me to address her graduate class at Kingsborough Community College - one of the City of New York (CUNY) colleges. - one of the City of New York (CUNY) colleges.

Suzanne thought it would be a good idea for her students to hear a genuine Rasta speak about our island and our culture, and it helped that I earned a paycheck for the pleasure of just talking about my life and beliefs. Suzanne said most of her students were Black, but had never seen anyone as 'awesome' as me.It was an experience that gave me a foundation for making other speeches.

In 2001 I was invited to Vienna, Austria, to speak at a conference on Caribbean culture organized by the great Austrian Professor Werner Zips, who has written several books on Jamaican and Rasta culture. The Conference was an important event, and Mutabaruka and I represented Rasta for 3 days. This was where I first met some of the growing body of 'White Rastas' and I took the opportunity to interview some of them and use the information to add a new chapter to my Rastafari book.

It was interesting to see Vienna, and I was especially

amazed to see the huge statues that are features of the city's buildings, carvings of men and women supporting the corners holding up the structure and decorating all over. It seemed like there must be several factories all over the city carving these giant monments and hundreds of stone masons whose solitary work was carving human bodies out of marble and stone.

Another speaking occasion was when the University of the US Virgin Islands invited me to address a conference on Rastafari and while there I got a chance to see what life was like on the smaller islands. It was unusual to be on such small islands and to see other islands floating close by in the sea that were not just little plots of land like we had offshore Jamaica and enjoyed for Sunday boat trips or adventure swime, but were 'foreign' territory belonging to other colonial masters such as France and England for which we would need a passport to visit.

I was taken on a day trip to St. John, one of the smaller US islands, where we hiked to the top of a hill for an event honouring slaves who had cast themselves off a precipice, rather than be returned to slavery, after an unsuccessful revolutionary attempt to take over the island.

In Curacao, another small Caribbean island where I was attending a World International Pre-Conference, I had a chance to visit the Kura Hulanda Museum where a wonderful collection of artefacts and memorabilia of the slave trade were exhibited in a beautiful space created by a Dutch millionaire.

It was also in Curacao where I was reminded of the old-style white racism, when I sat at an outside cafe hoping to have lunch and waited, waited, and waited until I realized that no waiter would take an order and I would not be served, as it was a 'whites-only' establishment. I smiled as I got up and looked for somewhere else to eat.

I made a solo trip to Fort Lauderdale, Florida, to hold a launch of my book "*Growing Out – Black Hair & Black Pride*" at the Fort Lauderdale Library, thanks to the help of Florida-Jamaican Tracy 'Marsh' Russell. It wasn't a large crowd, but an achievement nevertheless.

One nice trip was a return to London in 2012 to accept a Lifetime Achievement Award from the Black British Entertainment Film, Fashion and Television (BEFFTA) organization as a 'piomeer' of Black British journalism, thanks to a nomination by Black journalist Pauline Granston for my work as Britain's first Black television journalist. It was the first time I realised that my 1968 job was considered a breakthrough that was appreciated by British Blacks, and it was a great pleasure to receive this award because it showed that the pain I experienced in 1968 when racism brought an end to my job, was finally turned into a positive by the recognition of those for whom my job opened doors.

These days I am honoured in Britain's Black History Month every October for that achievement, so out of the pain came the pleasure of the Award and the recognition, which increases as years go by and more Black journalists follow in my footsteps.

It was a short visit, but I got to see my friends Anton and Judith Phillips again and see that London had not changed much. I was still glad I had not stayed.

The nicest US lecture trip of all was in 2016 to lecture to students and be the keynote speaker at the Texas Christian University, Honors Convocation at Forth Worth, Texas. It came from an invitation by TCU Professor of Religion Dr. Darren Middleton, who had first met me online when he interviewed me about my books and reviewed my novel *'Joseph - Rasta Reggae Fable'*. He wrote a great review of it in one of his books, *'Rastafari and the Arts'*, and we began an email friendship that continued for a few years.

Very knowledgeable about the Rastafari religion, Professor Middleton thought it was a good idea to expose his TCU students to a real life Rastafari, and to my great surprise and joy he invited me to spend a week at TCU speaking to several classes as well as staff members, with a highlight of my visit delivering the Honours Convocation speech, a major event on the University's end-of-semester activites.

I agreed to accept the TCU invitation if Makonnen could come with me, and the University agreed. However, what made the trip even more special was that when we told Professor Middleton that one of Makonnen's musical partners, the Jamaican DJ Rsenal D'Artillary, had moved to Houston and would love to see us while we were in Texas, he invited him to join us at TCU.

The three of us were treated like royalty for one week on the beautiful, modern TCU campus. We stayed in a lovely hotel, each with our own rooms, and each day a member of faculty hosted us at lunch or dinner at a special restaurant in the city.

I gave lectures to classes of students on various aspects of Rastafari - the philosophy, the music, the role of women and relationships, and explaining the spiritual belief, the importance of Selassie and how Rastafari was a modern and Black development of Christianity. As you can imagine, there were always very thoughtful questions and conversations with students after each lecture.

As a special event, Makonnen and Rsenal were invited to give a live performance of their reggae songs at the University's fabulous Pepsi Theatre to a crowded auditorium of students, for whom this was a rare opportunity to experience Jamaican reggae live. They went through their repertoire with zeal and the show became one of Makonnen's most special performance events. I also hosted the screening of Donisha Prendergast's film *"Rasta – A Soul Journey"* in which I am featured, an event that was screened to a packed auditorium.

My speech *"Dawta of JAH"* at the Honours Ceremony is reprinted towards the end of this book. The event was an impressive occasion, as to start the proceedings the school band performed a medly of Bob Marley songs, which was a lovely surprise for me. My speech was very well received, and I received many congratulations from the senior staff, provost and Chancellor when it ended.

After, I enjoyed being a special guest at the lavish

Graduation Dinner when academic prizes were presented. I remember meeting a brilliant student, Kelcie Gauntley, who won all the top prizes and her mother, both of whom have remained friends even now. It was a wonderful experience to be part of such a beautiful, progressive university and to have the opportunity to speak to and with the students, and best of all, I got paid for the pleasure of it.

I will always be indebted to Professor Darren Middleton for honouring me with such a wonderful invitation. My blessings to him, his wife Elizabeth and lovely son Jonathan.

We stayed on in Texas afterwards, flying to Houston to stay with Rsenal, his lovely wife Maryanita and their family, for two weeks and had a great time relaxing and enjoying Houston.

AFRICA AT LAST! THE WORLD CONFERENCE

As Makonnen grew, I continued to be an at-home mother, earning a small income by writing articles and columns in the daily newspapers. I also used the very-new internet to set up a website for a Rasta Information Service as an online space where I shared whatever news and information I could. As Rasta Information Service, I applied for and received Media Access to Rebel Salute and Reggae Sumfest and wrote about the events and the artists I met.

I thought that Rasta Information Service needed a publication, so I tried becoming a newspaper publisher myself, laying out and printing a 4-page colour tabloid *Rasta News* that I was certain would be a best seller.

I don't think I sold 10 copies. Every Rasta I offered it to said that since it was about Rasta, it should be free for them. I placed copies for sale at a popular Ital restaurant and hung around the Marley Museum yard trying to sell copies, but no luck. I tried a second edition, hoping some private sector company would see it as a useful medium for advertising, but no one did. I have just one copy of the first edition left.

I was sitting at home one day, writing articles for what I hoped would be a third edition of RASTA NEWS, when the phone rang.

"Mrs. Hannah, I am calling from Canada on behalf of

the United Nations. We have been trying to contact you for 3 weeks. We have money for you to buy your ticket to South Africa immediately to attend the World Conference Against Racism!"

I hardly remembered that I had applied as the Rasta Information Service to cover the World Conference because I was a Rasta journalist and Reparations was a major Rastafari call. I knew Reparations was going to be a major issue there and I deeply wanted to add my voice to the many voices I knew would be there, so I had applied. But it was almost like putting a message in a bottle and casting it out to sea with hope.

I had been inspired to fight for this particular Rastafari cause by the works of Jah Lloyd, a passionate Rastafari elder, artist and friend who had been the most outspoken Rasta on Reparations. Jah Lloyd had died a short while before, on his first trip to Africa, leaving a vacant space where action was badly needed. Speaking up about Reparations would be as if I was picking up his fallen banner and hoisting it high again.

I hardly thought my application would have been accepted, but it was! There was Thousands of Jamaican Dollars waiting for me and a flight booked to travel to Durban via London. I could hardly believe my good luck! My son was 15 and building a website for a major company, so I could safely leave him at home with his 'big man' friends to keep him company. I just had time to get a malaria shot and pack a bag.

I flew out immediately, arriving in Durban in the
midst of delegates from all over the world, people wearing
national dress of many styles and colours. Before leaving
Jamaica I had informed the Ministry of Foreign Affairs of my
invitation. To my great delight and honour, they invited me to
be an official member of the Jamaican delegation, glad to
have a Rasta in their group. I was greeted officially on arrival
at the conference center and given my Security ID entitiling
me to full access to the conference, its plenaries, meetings
and events. Senior Foreign Affairs official Sheila Monteith
(now an Ambassador) took me under her wing, explaining
what to do, while Jamaican Ambassador Stafford Neil greeted
me warmly.

Leading the Jamaican delegation was Ambassador
Dudley Thompson, one of the creators of the famous Abuja
Declaration and an international pioneer of the movement for
slavery Reparations, who was very well known in Africa and
Pan-African circles as the lawyer who defended Jomo
Kenyatta at his Mau Mau trials. I had known him from I was
a child, and he was glad to see me and proud of my
Afrocentric activities.

The Jamaican delegation's seats in the Conference
Assemby Hall were beside Japan, whose delegates hardly
showed up each day. To the left of their empty seats was the
delegation from Israel that included a brown-skinned lady,
who I assumed was one of the many Ethiopians who had
migrated to Israel. I wore my white Ethiopian dresses and
shama headwraps every day, so on the first day the lady

greeted me in Amharic, confirming my assumption that she was Ethiopian. I had to smile and tell her I was Jamaican and my Amharic was very limited, but she had heard of Rastafari, so I began a very amicable relationship with the Israeli delegation thereafter.

A problem that kept arising at the Conference was that every debate on every topic on the agenda soon brought the issue of Reparations to the surface and when this problem eventually seemed likely to derail the entire Conference, the topic of Reparations was moved into a new plenary containing the most passionate African and Caribbean supporters of Reparations, as well as the representatives of European enslaving nations who were being called to answer.

Ambassador Thompson and I were delegated to represent Jamaica in this plenary and found myself in company with delegates from the Caribbean including Ras Iral Jabari and Hilary Beckles of Barbados, as well as delegates from Africa. The plenary contained many angry verbal confrontations between representatives of the Black people who had been enslaved and the White people who had enslaved us, with many attempts to bargain for commitments from the White nations, which they were determined not to give.

It was a hard struggle, but by the end we finally managed to agree on what should be included in the Conference's statement on Reparations. I am proud to report that at my insistence, with support from Ambassador Thompson, we were able to have the list of Forms of

Reparations include a special recognition of Reparations with Repatriation and the words: *"The Welcomed return and re-settlement in Africa of descendants of enslaved Africans"* were added as the very last item on that important and historic list.

Being in Africa was a special and wonderful experience and Durban was beautiful. It was good to see Black people moving about in control of such a developed city, just as it was shocking for me to pass poor, ragged White people begging at the stop lights. Jamaica seemed so far away!

To have touched my feet on the Motherland was very special to me. It hit me the hardest one night as I sat in a speaker's tent at the People's Village outside the Conference Center, looking down at my feet on the red earth of Durban and seeing how different it was to any earth I had seen at home in Jamaica. It was African earth, I realised. I was here in Africa with my feet on the earth of my ancestors! I really had to think about that.

As I was thinking, a woman with her head covered in a flowing scarf came into the tent, saw us and came over to us with tears streaming down her face. She bowed down before us, saying over and over "Thank you for coming to South Africa my Sister! Thank you for coming to South Africa my brother! Thank you for coming to South Africa!!!" I looked at her, but she wasn't mad. She really meant it. "Thank you for coming!"

Tears rolled down my face and my heart was

overwhelmed by the fact that it was many, many generations ago that people related to me had lived in Africa, had touched their feet to this African earth, but had never known me, their stolen daughter. I cried for all the family in Africa I had never met, and I cried for the family who had been taken to Jamaica who I also had never met.

I felt alone and lonely, my mother and father were dead, I had no more link with Africa. All I had now to link me with Africa was my son. I hoped I had made the African blood in his multi-racial mixture strong enough to endure and keep the link alive.

Heading into the Conference Center in the morning that the Final Report was presented, walking towards me was the Conference Chairman, UN Ambassador Mary Robinson, former Prime Minister of Ireland. To my surprise, as we passed each other she looked me in the eyes with a smile and winked. It wasn't till I saw the Conference daily newspaper a little later that I realised she knew who I was because she had seen my photo on the paper's front page in an interview in which I had said: "I am the first member of my family to have touched foot in Africa for 300 years. I cried when I arrived. We need Reparations so we can return home."

The World Conferencee Against Racism turned out to be an unofficial sitting of the United Nations, as senior diplomats and politicians of every country were present. Of them all, the presence of Fidel Castro was the most historic, but the most newsworthy personality was Madeline Albright, the US Secretary of State who headed the American delegation that the world had expected Colin Powell to lead. The fight against racism took another road at the Conference in an incident that made big news – the walkout of the US and Israeli delegations after disagreeing with the continued hammering of a resolution that equated Zionism with racism.

In a co-incidence that needs to go on record, the walkout took place at the same time as a meeting I had arranged - with approval of Ambassador Neil - for the Israeli delegation to formally meet with the Jamaican delegation to discuss ways I believed Jamaica could help in bringing a peaceful resolution to the Palestinian situation. As we sat waiting, Ambassador Neil's phone rang cancelling the meeting without giving a reason.

We all left the meeting room and went to the lift – only to find as the doors opened that we had to step back to give way to Madeline Albright and her US delegation walking out of the Conference!!

Yes, it was that kind of Conference.

Leaving Durban, the flight stopped at Cape Town en route to London. An hour later they informed us that the flight was cancelled and would be re-scheduled for 2 days later. I was tired and sad to be away from my son for so long. I cried.

A kind airline person booked me into a lovely hotel suite and I woke the next morning with a beautiful view across the sea to Robben Island where Nelson Mandela had been imprisoned. Then the kind lady booked me on a flight that day to Fort Lauderdale, telling me the only problem was that it took 17 hours. It was the longest flight I have ever held my breath for, but I was glad to be going home.

Arriving in the USA, the immigration officer tried to put me through the usual delays and irritations they always do, but I couldn't take it this time. I just stood and bawled out loudly: "I have been away from my child for two weeks! I will miss my connection!!!

A woman looking like just another passenger leaned up off a wall and gave a special signal to the immigration officer, who waved me on just in time to catch my plane to Kingston. My son was glad to see me. I went to bed and fell asleep immediately.

I was still deep in slumber next morning when I was awakened by my son shouting and calling me to the television. There before our eyes a plane flew into the Twin Towers, and exploded in flames. Minutes later another one did!!!

It was 9/11 – the most famous day in aviation history!

In the global crisis that followed, all air travel was halted for days. I would have been stuck somewhere in the world for days, if I had not taken the 17 hour flight back home.

I have always wondered if it was mere coincidence that 9/11 happened after the US delegation walked out of the World Conference Against Racism!

Looking back through my collection of documents, flyers, posters and information from 20 years ago, I find it hard to believe that so little has happened that so many good people worked so hard to achieve in Durban. Racism is still a monster devouring the hearts and lives of Black people everywhere, reaching from the poorest to the highest families. The war for Reparations for Caribbean slavery is still being fought with no end in sight, though the enslavers monuments are being destroyed, one by one.

Despite all that, the World Conference was a bright light along our path and a lifeline onto which we can still hold firmly today, however much we fear it is weak and will break.

Let us press on, brave soldiers, let us press on!

A luta continua!

We SHALL overcome!

REPARATIONS

Coming home after the WCAR, I set up an online website on Reparations connecting those of us and the organizations who had been at WCAR. In time I built this into the Jamaica Reparations Movement, J.A.R.M., an online group of international reparationists especially Caribbean and American, including such members as as Ras Iral Jabari, Charles Ogletree and Randall Robinson, using the website and email to try and build the movement for Reparations in Jamaica.

This becan my intensive unpaid work to generate interest in the matter of Reparations, whose just cause had been endorsed by the United Nations in Durban. As well as the website, I spent my time writing articles, Letters to the Editor, making calls and giving interviews to journalists and radio stations. My most important action was creation of a Petition seeking signatures for the call for Reparations that I carried around with me to where people who should be interested in supporting Reparations were expected to be.

To my surprise, there was little support, especially not from those I thought would have stepped forward in strong numbers, especially in the Rastafari community. I know that in their hearts they all supported Reparations, especially as a fund for Repatriation.

But they didn't come forward with verbal and personal support for either of the two public events I organized, or the many letters and articles I wrote in the local newspapers and online. Certainly no financial support.

The only money I ever got for my work on Reparations was from the White English lawyer and defender of both reparations and ganja legalizaton, Lord Anthony Gifford who saw me one day waiting for a bus and offered me a ride. When I told him I had been delivering an article to the GLEANER on Reparations, he gave me Five Thousand Dollars, a huge amount of money in those days.

Other than that, I was on my own. All my work on Reparations came out of my very small pocket. I wasn't expecting payment, I didn't even see the financial possibility of the colonizing nations ever paying for slavery. But I didn't expect to be the only person doing the work. I was sure everyone was an enthusiastic about the topic, as I.

One person who gave help was Verene Shepherd, then Professor of History at the University of the West Indies, who invited me to speak on Reparations to a class of her students. I asked her to arrange in return for me to give a lecture at UWI and she did, arranging for me to use the Neville Hall Lecture Theatre and hosting an event in 2003.

I put out a public invitation and made some special invitations. Most important of all, I created a Reparations Document, a brochure featuring a full explanation of a proper Jamaican claim for Reparations. It included a Solemn Declaration, the Fundamental Objectives, the Forms of

Reparations, Structural Proposals, and the Plan of Action, all creating the Public Statement of Jamaica's Claims for Reprations.

About 30 people came, including my great friend Pearnel Charles, the MP, who had just been honoured as an African Chief. He brought with him fellow MP Mike Henry, who had recently proposed a Parliamentary debate on ganja legalization, and Pearnel told Mike Henry to add Reparations to his debate and take them both to Parliament, which he did, beginning his ongoing support of Reparations.

Approved by the 30 persons gathered, the J.A.R.M Reparations Document became the historic foundation of the Government of Jamaica's decision to take Parliamentary action officially for Reparations. It was quite an achievement to have finally put Jamaica's claim in writing and to have it approved by so many people from so many different sources. Rastas of differing Mansions, Garveyite Sister Mariam Samaad, poets, teachers, students, writers and Jamaicans. I was proud.

In 2004 I published a Rastafari Invoice for Repatriation with Reparations issued by the J.A.R.M. that gained international publicity

While working with then-Minister of Culture Babsy Grange in 2007, the matter of Reparations came on her agenda and I submitted the J.A.R.M. Document to her as the basis of what could be proposed by Jamaica. She approved it and also my list of persons to set up a Parliamentary Committee chaired by Prof. Barry Chevannes to discuss the way forward on Reparations, based on the J.A.R.M.'s proposals. The first person I recommended was Prof. Verene Shepherd, who had been such an important help to me when I held the important J.A.R.M. Meeting. She proved to be the right person and has continued taking forward the struggle for Reparations since that appointment.

The Committee's recommendations were accepted and then moved forward to a Parliamentary Debate led by MP Mike Henry where Reparations was finally accepted and approved. I was praised in the Debate by 4 MPs for the work of the J.A.R.M. and I was satisfied that all my hard work had an appropriate result. It was good to see action that would continue the work that was started in Durban.

The work continues today through the setting up of a National Comissionl on Reparations and I am glad to have played a major role in making Jamaica's claim become stronger. Europe needs constant reminders of the evil they did and its after-effects. Only their humble apology and genuine acknowledgement of how their evil enabled them to enrich their nations, can end the perpetual racism built on the attitude of White Superiority over the Black race that was practised with such horror and brutality in chattel slavery.

But frankly, I don't think we will ever get Reparations – certainly not in the way Rastafari envisages it, namely as a big lump sum to pay for Repatriation to Africa for those who desire it, and their Resettlement. Those now heading the Reparations movement ask for other forms of payment like health care and education, or funding from foundations, corporations and universities donated by those that recognize their guilt and debt. But payment for Repatriation is not mentioned often.

What has not come is an apology from the many countries, organizations and families that benefited from slavery. Without that, nothing has changed except wider recognition of the debt due and the negative results of slavery that still remain. Those from whom an apology must come have perfected the act of never giving one.

What must come, instead, is an acknowledgement of the evils of White Supremacy, and an elevation of the ideals of Black Supremacy in which we have built a new world on the ashes we have inherited, without looking back, only forward. The Black Lives Matter movement is here at the right time to start setting that business right.

I no longer work for Reparations. To me, it's a waste of time because if any European nation was to truly pay the debt of slavery, it would bankrupt their nation out of existence. They see this even more clearly than I can, and European governments know their people will vote them out of power if they agree to pay Black people any large sum of Reparations out of their taxes.

A friend said I should apply to Thames Television for reparations to repay me for the income I lost when their bowing to racism caused me to lose the job and potential income. But 50 years later I see how many doors have been opened for Black British journalists, who ignore the block and kick the door open wider because I already did it as their example. When they praise me as a 'pioneer', a 'role model' and a 'living legend', for opening the door for them, I realise in the end I got the best reward and I smile to see lemonade made out of lemons. There is no reason for me to look back.

In the same way, perhaps instead of looking back at the very bad history that brought us to today, we could spend our energies looking at how much better we are now years later than our former colonizers. With all the money they have, their societies are a nightmare of crime, racism, child abuse, poor health, race wars, bad weather ... I could go on.

Meantime, Jamaica is envied as the most wonderful place on earth to be. Great music, great beaches, great mountains, great food, great sportsmen, great people. Everyone wants to be in Jamaica, people even wish they were Jamaicans. If only we knew how great Jamaica is, we would spend all our time building up our beautiful country to become a showplace, a living theme park and an example to the world that would end all the crime that is born in poverty.

The murders would end when we learn LOVE instead of hate. That's the kind of Reparations we need, the repair of the beautiful island that was handed over in 1834 with no compensation to the people who built it, the people who hacked out its forests into farms and villages, made roads out of dirt tracks and river banks, who planted food to feed themsleves and built houses out of wattle and daub to live in, and who gave thanks at the end of their labours to relax and swim in the clean rivers and the warm seas on white sand beaches. It's ours now, and it's not even started to be as beautiful in every way, as it could be

Look at where we are coming from 250 years after the end of slavery, from absolutely nothing to a modern nation proud of the accomplishments over decades of history of our famous citizens, too many to name and proud creators of a new world religion, a new music and a new lifestyle culture.

So much money has been spent on salaries, lawyers, seminars, conferences, air fares and more, paying people to look for Reparations. The search looks likely to continue for many more decades. Is it worth it?

Jamaican reparations were certainly due to the Rastafari survivors of the infamous Coral Gardens Incident, so while working as Cultural Liaison to Minister of Culture Babsy Grange, I advised her that it was time to offer an apology and provide reparatory funding to the survivors. I was glad to help make this happen after two years of work and negotiations, and I was also able to get Government to set up a home for the most needy Elders. More is still to come to repair that wrong.

Instead of looking backwards to slavery and those who enslaved us, I prefer to look forward to build a future, as the Emperor advised Ethiopians to do after the defeat of the Italians. He said there should be no recrimination, no revenge.

"Instead, we must put to the best use the rich heritage of our past for, in that way, and in that way alone can we live to the highest standard set by our forefathers. We hope the future generations will realize the magnitude of

sacrifices that were required to accomplish all the works, so that they may preserve it as gain.

"Africans have been reborn as free men. The blood that was shed and the sufferings that were endured, are today Africa's advocates for freedom and unity. The glories and advantages of freedom cannot be purchased with all the world's material wealth."

I don't need any Reparations.

THE GANJA CAMPAIGN

The one Rasta campaign that I have never stopped working on is the legalization of ganja.

After leaving the campaign for Reparations in the hands of the Jamaican government, I reassumed my interest in the work being done to change the laws against growing and use of ganja. Ganja advocacy has always been a major issue of mine because I am a Rasta.

For a start, I smoked ganja freely and though discretly breaking the law daily, at no time did I consider myself a criminal. I knew the power ganja holds to focus my mind on thoughts on higher realms, and I acknowledged ganja as my religious sacrament that keeps me in touch with the Divinity of JAH within me.

As a committed Rasta, I had started using my pen to challenge the Ganja laws in the early 1970s and by the 1990s a few people of like mind became bold enough to come together and form an organization to confront the system, The Legalize Ganja Group.

We few were lawyers Sandra 'Sajoya' Alcott, Lord Anthony Gifford and Antoinette Haughton, author and UWI lecturer Dr. Dennis Forsythe, Ras DaSilva, labour leader of the KSAC City Cleansing Department and myself as the two Rasta members, and Chinese-Jamaican architect Paul Chang.

We wrote Letters to the newspapers and took every opportunity speak on radio, television and in public about how unfair the law was and how much money could be made from legalizing the herb.

The Legalize Ganja group grew silent as members died or moved abroad. But I continued my campaign to bring about realistic changes in the law. We watched, as slowly the government started discussons about the decriminalization of ganja. I attended as many of the meetings as I could, and participated whenever the crowd of speakers allowed me space for a comment. I also continued writing in the press and now on social media, such as Facebok.

One action I am proud of was the formation of an online group, the Jamaican People's Cannabis Development Council to circulate a Petition asking that Government institute a process in the new law to wipe the records of people convicted for personal possession of ganja. It was a good proposal and the Government made it a first step in its actions towards legalization.

In addition, the Petition included other proposals for setting up the ganja industry and to handle the establishment of ganja businesses and taxation to benefit the economy, enabling producers to sell their products where legal in Jamaica or abroad.

It was good to see the work the Government was finally doing to legalize ganja. It was as if to compensate for the great disappointment of the Socialist Seventies when we all hoped Michael Manley would legalize ganja, the PNP

Government did what was necessary to do the right thing this time.

Guided by the steady leadership of then-Minister of Justice Mark Golding and with the help of PNP firebrand Paul Burke who had been the silent strength behind the PNP for decades, the Government held two years of meetings, consultations and forums in which Jamaicans of all kinds got a chance to say what they wanted and criticize what they didn't like, to ensure the bands of Jamaica's ganja laws were finally broken.

Though Rastafari had fought since its inception for Jamaica to take the step, Jamaica waited until America confronted their own federal laws and legalized the growing and use of ganja in many different ways in many different States, setting good examples for us to follow. Senator Golding held firmly to the boundaries of international law and the binding UN Convention that had so far prevented the legal growing and sale of ganja, while he carefully revised the Dangerous Drugs Law to establish the foundation of a medical marijuana business.

There were many good, active voices in this process. I must call the names of Dickie Crawford of the Ganja Growers & Producers Association, Kathy Lennon – Jamaica's leading female ganja grower, music executive Maxine Stowe (whose claim to speak for the entire Rastafari community as leader of the 'Millenium Council' was always disputed), and Dr. Henry Lowe who had produced several ganja-based products including Canasol for glaucoma and Asmasol for asthma.

There were international voices such as Americans Josh Stanley, whose family had bred the miraculous Charlotte's Web strain for children with epilepsy, and Professor Charles Nesson of Harvard Law School, who brought links with the famous ganja magazine High Times.

The meetings were full of high voltage energy, loud interventions and even some wild suggestions, but it was an exciting time to see the opening of the doors to the Green Gold industry we Rastas had always been agitating for.

I felt the widespread celebration at the Parliamentary announcement of the changes to the Dangerous Drugs Act, but I could see that the euphoria would soon subside as people realized that nothing had really changed and that instead some changes are still necessary in the new law.

Yes, Government says it's now OK for me to carry 2 ounces (how much is that?) of Ganja on my person, but the person who will be growing more than that amount to supply my 2 ounces will still be breaking the law against growing Ganja without a License, so the small vendor is not included in the plans! Nothing has changed there. He is still criminalized! Ganja is not decriminalized for him unless he has an official License to grow that ganja.

Further, dashing hopes of those who planned to open an 'irie' business where people could relax and smoke their 2 ounces of Ganja, the Cabinet witholds from Ganja smokers the rights it gives cigarette smokers to have designated public smoking areas except in licensed 'herb houses', nowhere else. Why the double standard?

And what about tourists – they want to be allowed 2 ounces too, but Mark Golding's Cabinet (and the JLP one that followed it) have not freed Ganja smoking for 'recreational' purposes. That means those times when I'm just chilling on a beach, or relaxing with friends or anything else that is neither 'sacramental' or 'medical', I will be breaking the law. It looks to me like it's still illegal to chill and smoke some Ganja!

I also forsee the great problem that has arisen for Government to decide who is a Rasta and thereby allowed to smoke Ganja 'sacramentally'. How is 'sacramental smoking' defined? If Government proposes to be the authority to identify, decide and register Rasta 'sacramental spaces', how will Rastas be identified to apply for such designations, unless they do what they should have done long ago, and register their membership as Rastas in Mansion databases that don't yet exist?

If every Rasta is entitled, Rastas may be able to declare their homes, their cars, their businesses places, their open lots as 'sacramental spaces'!

I also want to see the inclusion of a major Government-sponsored Rasta business in the institutions now being set up, in recognition of the role Rasta has played in keeping alive the "Legalize It' campaign for more than 8 decades. This is a debt that is owed to the Rasta community in memory of those who have gone before us and are no longer here. Instead, it is clear that the persons who will help build a Jamaican cannabis industry are not any of the original Rasta planters, growers and users.

The revision of the law includes, most importantly, recognition of Rastafari declaration that ganja is the sacrament of our religion, as important as wine is to the Catholic religion. The recognition gives Rastas the right to use ganja personally within legally defined boundaries and at Rastafari gatherings such as Nyabinghi. We can even organize events where ganja can be smoked.

Having given Rastas the right use ganja, the revised Act also declares that every Jamaican is now free to grow 5 plants of ganja each. A good move that few people act on, but while we can grow 5 plants for ourselves, what if those 5 plants grow more than we need personally. Can we sell the surplus to Government for it to process and sell to earn national income?

One important thing I think the law is incomplete until it is revised to include it, is the original Jamaican People's Cannabis Development Council proposal that Taxes earned by the ganja industry be used to finance a FREE national health service for Jamaica. At present the tax income is designated for use by the ineptly named National Council for Drug Abuse. If we are allowed to grow ganja for medicine, let the income be used to care for our people's need for medical care.

Rastafari Elder Bongo Daniel, the greatest Nyabinghi Harpsist (drummer) Rastafari has ever known, died sick and old in a house with no electricity, no medicine, no food. That was a sad day for me, because I had no money to help him and he deserved much better for all he had done for Rastafari and for Jamaica.

Too many Rastafari Elders like him are dying without money for health care. These are the same Rasta Elders who kept growing and smoking Ganja, no matter what Babylon said, keeping the industry alive under much local and international pressure. These are the same Rasta Elders who gave Jamaica its famous and lucrative Rasta Culture based on ganja. They deserve our care in their old age.I think the opening of the Jamaican ganja industry must incorporate a FREE Jamaican National Health Service.

So, did they 'legalize it'? Not enough, as far as I can see. Wiping the records was the ace card and the cost of restoring one's good name was kept to a minimum, as an apology for the hurt and suffering the law has caused so many. Another good thing is that the proposals to decriminalize have set some things free, including the congested courts, jails and prisons.

The revised Dangerous Drugs Act is not everything we wanted, such as the free use of ganja for 'recreational use', or even the very optimistic hope that those already involved for years in the illegal industry could be able to continue doing so without restriction. An ambitious hope. But Senator Mark Golding and PNP activst Paul Burke must be given overwhelming credit for opening the door wide for what we Rastas had been asking, begging and marching for over the decades.

We Rastafari would have loved to hear that decriminalization will bring us new strains of Sensimilia developed to replace that famous strain that was wiped out in the 70s, when the Jamaica Police and Army enthusiastically helped wage the US 'war against drugs' with helicopters and spraying across the island.

But in the end I am glad to see that on the Rastafari side, the final document details the rights and benefits that Rastafari will receive under decriminalization and/or legalization. They can't take that away from us. The battle we were fighting from the Seventies to today has finally been won.

"Legalize it and I will advertise it", sang Peter Tosh. We did our part and we are still doing that in songs that continue Peter's work.

MY BOOKS

I am a writer and my life has been always about writing, so I write. Newspaper articles, columns, Letters, speeches, proposals, film scripts, advertising copy, press releases, news stories, feature stories, entertainment stories, book reviews, album reviews, celebrity interviews. Anything that has needed to be written, I write it and earn my living by doing that.

I knew I was supposed to write at least one book in my life, to earn the right to call myself an author, so I wrote five.

*

'Rastafari – the New Ceation', first published in 1980, was not the first book I wrote, though it was the first published. *'GROWING OUT- Black Hair & Black Pride'* was the first, written in the months after I came home from England in 1972 when I knew the history of my life in England was unique and needed to be told before I forgot it all. Little did I know that we never forget such memories. So I typed out as much as I could remember and then packed it away in a big envelope and stored it safely.

In 2010 Arif Ali, a Guyanese businessman who published a weekly Black newspaper I used to write for in London, asked me to write a chapter for a picture book on Jamaica he was publishing and I showed him the *'Growing*

Out' manuscript. As someone who knew me from my days in England when I wrote columns for his Black newspaper and who respected the history I had made in my job as Britain's first TV journalist, he agreed to have his Hansib Publications publish it in England and market it internationally, so it was finally published for everyone to read.

My good girlfriend Beverly Anderson Manley who I went to England with and shared a flat and many laughs when we lived there, agreed to be guest speaker at the book launch which was a major favour, and the Bob Marley Museum let me hold the Launch there. Both big names helped me get attention and reviews in the local media and the book was distributed by Novelty Trading Company to all the pharmacies and bookselling outlets they controlled island-wide, and online at Amazon.com.

After two years Hansib announced the book was sold out and they were re-printing. As I had not received any royalties from that printing, I wrote Hansib asking about that, but months later I received a reply simply saying that there were 200 copies of the book waiting for me to collect them and that was all. I got a friend in London to pick them up from Hansib and then I decided to take hold of publishing under my own company Jamaica Media Productions Ltd. I uploaded to Amazon a copy of the book that I had approved for the earlier edition, and found myself both and author and publisher once again.

In 2020 publicity about a British Press award named after me caught the attention of the great Black British author and Booker Prize winner Bernardine Evaristo. She did some research about me, discovered GROWING OUT and brought it to the attention of her publishers, Penguin UK to be published in a series she edited of Black British writers.

I can never thank Bernardine enough for doing that and giving new life to my story and my career as a writer. That someone who is such a great writer should take time to give attention to another writer, is one of the greatest acts of Christly LOVE I have ever experienced, and I pray for continued blessings for this wonderful woman.

*

'Joseph – a Rasta Reggae Fable' is my literary tribute to Bob Marley and my early Rasta teachers. After Bob died, all the foreign journalists who had met him started writing books about him and reggae music, using their good connections in the international media and entertainment worlds to get published.

However, I always noticed that Bob's story as a Rasta and his Rasta way of life was missing from all the accounts by people who could only see, but not overstand just what Rasta was and what made Bob's life different because he was a Rasta. It seemed that side of Bob was never mentioned.

I remembered the friendship I had with Bob and what it meant to me growing as a Rasta. In 1992 when my son was 3, long after Bob passed from the flesh, the memories were so vivid that I decided to write a novel with a hero just like Bob and a story with all those memories that would be told from a Rasta perspective.

I gave the story a female narrator and started each chapter with a Bible verse that indicated where the story would go. The book had twelve chapters – a number I considered spiritually appropriate – and I hired an artist friend Thorold DeMercado to draw twelve pictures to illustrate each chapter.

I was sure my book would be a best-seller and give me money to live on forever, without ever having to take a nine-to-five job again. It didn't achieve that objective by any means, but every month or so I get a royalty check from Amazon that I can spend at the supermarket.

'*Joseph*' was first published in 1992 and has since had four editions, each with a unique cover art. Some of the comments about it show how well it was received, the best of which was written by Joe Jurgensen, the man with the largest collection of books about Bob and his music, who wrote:

"Not all Bob Marley books are biographies, photography or songbooks. One in particular that does not really fit into any category is "Joseph – A Rasta Reggae Fable." As the title suggests it is a fable about Joseph, a fictional musician from the Third World who rises up to worldwide fame only to ride off into the African sunset'.

After robust sales in Jamaica through distribution by Novelty Trading Company, British publishers McMillan Caribbean agreed to publish an international edition. It took two years from contract signing to publication, but eventually I found myself again with no royalties, so once again I published a digital edition via JamaicaMedia Productions at

Amazon, where it is still available.

*

My next book *"HOME THE FIRST SCHOOL – A Homeschooling Guide To Early Childhood Education"* was written to share with curious parents what home-schooling was all about. When I decided to continue home-schooling my son instead of sending him to a traditional school, it was considered a shocking thing to do. Despite people being amazed at the fact that Makonnen could read so well as such an early age and knew so much about so many topics, they thought I was mad to be teaching him myself. *"HOME THE FIRST SCHOOL"* was the book in which I explained what I was doing, how I did it and why.

When Makonnen was appointed Youth Technology Consultant to the Jamaican Government in 1998 at age 13 years, the Jamaican public suddenly realised that home-schooling was a viable education option, especially as home-schooled children were becoming famous for winning international competitions like the Spelling Bee and getting college scholarships at an early age. Makonnen became an instant national celebrity and remains remembered by all Jamaica, even though that was so many years ago.

I published the book in 2009 with a small number of print copies and, as usual, made copies available at Amazon in print and Kindle editions. This is still my most popular book, and as some of the links no longer exist 20 years later, I recently updated it in a new edition subtitled *"How To Grow A Genius Child"* also available at Amazon.

Self-publishing at Amazon is a true innovation for writers, as we no longer have to wait for publishers to decide to give birth to your book before it can reach readers. I can promote my books myself and earn my royalties from checks paid directly into my bank account. I like it this way.

*

"The Moon Has Its Secrets" is my second novel, inspired by the life of National Heroine, the Maroon warrior called Nanny. I was greatly inspired to write it because of two books I had read.

The first one *"Women Who Run with the Wolves"* by Dr. Clarissa Pinkola Estés explains that "...*within every woman there lives a powerful force, filled with good instincts, passionate creativity, and ageless knowing. Women Who Run with the Wolves, unfolds rich intercultural myths, fairy tales, folk tales, and stories ... to help women reconnect with the fierce, healthy, visionary attributes of this instinctual nature.*"

I identified greatly with the 'wild women' of this deeply spiritual book, constantly holding on to that remnant of wildness that being a Rasta enables me to live proudly.

The second book was *"The Maroon Story"*, by Beverly Carey, a treasure trove of Jamaican history with special emphasis on the Maroons, the fierce runaway slaves who carved a life for themselves in the wild Jamaican jungles free from the plantation to live in nature as they had done in Africa. As I read it, I found myself thinking about the story of our National Heroine Nanny of the Maroons, the only female considered great enough to be included among five male heroes.

Nanny certainly ran with the wolves, refusing to be civilized as a slave but choosing instead to live free in the mountains and wage war against the British enslavers. Who was she? What was her story? We know little about her, yet we made her Jamaica's highest woman. I saw a story that was hers, that was mine, that was every Jamaican woman who had set foot on this island as a slave.

The story flowed from my fingers as if they didn't belong to me. As it unfolded, there were days when I didn't know where it would go or what would happen next. I felt as if there was an unseen spirit guiding the story along and putting words under my fingertips, making the characters go where they were supposed to go. The book had a life of its own.

Sometimes, even today, I look at the words and wonder how I wrote them, how I knew to write those scenes, how the story's characters developed, what they said. The river and the waterfall that is so important in the story are so real, yet I have never seen it or been there in all the exploring I did while living in Portland. That book is very special for me.

So these are my five books, and you now hold in your hand my sixth.

MY FILMS

I have always loved films. Like everyone else, I learned about life from Hollywood films. From growing up at the Carib, Tropical, Odeon, Palace and other Jamaican cinemas, I was a dedicated fan of films, film stars and film making.

In my late teen years when I started grown-up life working as a Kingston secretary, two young British film makers donated by the British Council to help set up the main Jamaican TV station and government film service, started a film club showing some good foreign films never seen in Jamaica. It was good to be among them seeing films and talking about film making. Being a member of the club gave me a headstart on the wide variety of films I was able to see when I moved to live in London.

Going to the movies in London was my special treat. Not only could I see all the major feature films, but also the wide variety of foreign films that became popular in the Sixties. Films by French film makers Francois Truffaut, Jean-Luc Goddard and Jacques Demy, Italian Michaelangelo Antonio, the Swede Ingmar Bergman and Poland's Roman Polanski, as well as films by a new genre of young British film makers and actors, gave me a bountiful buffet from which to fill my hunger for films of all kinds.

In London my film friends included Ismael Merchant and James Ivory, the partners of Merchant-Ivory Films that burst onto the international film scene with their groundbreaking black-and-white feature *"Shakespeare Wallah"* about an English theatrical family that travels around India giving performances of Shakespeare's plays.

Ismael was a high-class Indian who loved to host dinner parties at the high-class Indian restaurants in London, and I enjoyed their company and some great dinners many evenings. James recently won his first Oscar, but Ismael passed some years ago. They were just two of the many film actors and directors who I met as part of the Swinging London scene.

From 1968 till I left in 1972 I worked at several British TV stations filming and making programmes. My jobs included writing the story, speaking it live or on film, interviewing subjects, supervising the editing of footage, and checking the finished story. It therefore follows to reason that I wanted to make my own films.

My first chance was as a Jury member of the Leipzig Film Festival in 1978. The festival producers arranged for the GDR (German Democratic Republic) TV station to assign me a cameraman and a sound recordist, and I was given free reign to interview anyone I wished and to use clips from films I requested. This was very good fortune. I was delighted.

I called my film *"The Peaceful Gun"* using the

festival's motto of 'Films of the World for the Peace of the World" highlighting the many countries where East Germany was helping the African revolutionary wars in Rhodesia, Angola and South Africa, and supporting the Palestian cause against Israel. I interviewed Cuban film makers who had been filming in Angola, South African teenagers who were anti-apartheid warriors, an Israeli who supported the Palestinian cause, and an old Vietnamese man who was part of the opposition to the American war.

When the film festival was finished, they arranged for me to have 2 days in the GDR-TV editing rooms to put together the film. In those days film was made using separate rolls of vision and sound. Both were edited simultaneously, with cuts being stuck together with sticky tape, then after a final decision on the finished edit, the two tapes needed to be 'married' into one tape.

This was a long, and expensive, process that I could not do in East Germany, so I brought the tapes home to Jamaica and asked for Government help to 'marry' them. The Government said my trip was not 'official', so I could not use official resources. As I could not afford to pay for the process, I put the tapes at the back of my closet and looked for a job. Some time later an American friend offered to have the tapes married at a film studio in New York and I gave them to her. Never heard from her or about my film since.

*

My second film had better luck. As I wrote earlier, on a 1982 trip to England to promote my book *"Rastafari – The New Creation"*, Jeremy Isaacs - the former producer of the TV progamme I used to work on - was now heading a brand new TV channel designed to provide more options to feature England's diverse communities. He invited me to make a one-hour documentary on my view of England ten years after having left to return to Jamaica and live a Rastafari life.

The film was *"Race, Rhetoric, Rastafari"* and it was shown in the opening months of the new channel. In it I got a chance to criticise England and especially the British media for not doing more to end racism. I interviewed some people who could give a deeper view of the situation: the Black actor Anton Phillips, of whose children I was godmother; leading TV interviewer Joan Bakewell (now a Dame); Tessa Topolski, sister of my friend Daniel and daughter of the famous artist Feliks Topolski; Arif Ali, Guyanese editor of Black newspaper Caribbean Times, and two Rastafari – one a woman wishing she could find a way home, and another a musician with the group Ras Messengers.

I got permission to use some reggae music on soundtrack, including my favourite scene in *"The Harder They Come"* and some music by Ras Messengers, I-JahMan Levi and the Rastafarians. I filmed in Birmingham and was surprised to see that the children who had been babies when I worked at ATV-Birmingham, had now grown up into the Rastafari teenagers I saw all around the city.

The film was shown in the opening weeks of the new channel and can now be seen on YouTube.

*

Returning to Jamaica and my father's home in Port Antonio, I got a new job as director of public relations for the College of Agriculture that had recently been opened at a beautiful new location in the lush parish of Portland. The closure of the school at its previous location near Kingston had been controversial and the new location was considered 'too far away'. My job was to bring information to the public about the new school and its great rural location, and at the same time give the students a sense of belonging.

I came up with the idea of teaching the students how to make a film by having the students perform all parts of the film-making process. They had to come up with the concept idea, write the script, cast the performers and become the film crew. My job was to teach each of them their jobs and produce the finished film.

We selected three female students to be the featured actors, we filmed stories from each girl about why they were studying agriculture, and I showed a group of male students how to operate the camera and sound equipment. Our finished film "*By The Land We Live*" was shown on the government educational TV programming, and the College of Agriculture was proud to be featured nationally in an unusual and interesting way.

*

I got married soon thereafter, gave birth to my son Makonnen, and didn't get to make another film until he was seven years old. We were in Montego Bay, when a good friend who fell in love with Makonnen gave us a present of a week's stay at a hotel in Orcabessa that catered specially to families with children.

The Boscobel Beach Club was owned by the Issa family, well known for being pioneers in the Jamaican hotel industry. We had a most wonderful week at Boscobel and hotelier Zein Issa also fell in love with Makonnen. I was working in Kingston as secretary to Errol O'Mealy, a music producer and husband to top reggae artist J.C. Lodge, who also allowed me to bring Makonnen to his studio and gave him free rein to play with the instruments and machines.

One day Makonnen said to me: "Mom, why don't we make a movie at Boscobel Beach about a group of kids who find a treasure map and go looking for it." I thought this was an impossible dream, but Makonnen persisted that I could write such a script and make a movie. Not only did he make the suggestion, but he turned to an electric keyboard in the music room and played a tune.

"Here is the theme song for it," he declared, singing a chorus: *"Oh it could be so nice, living in a Kids Paradise..."*

That's how the first of my two *'KIDS PARADISE"* films happened, and Makonnen's first song produced.

It wasn't hard to write a script. I thought it would be more difficult to persuade the hotel to let us film there, and moreover, what about a budget! But when I called Zein Issa to ask permission, she not only said we could use Boscobel Beach, but gave me a budget to make the film as a promotion for the hotel.

Next we looked for the children to act in the film. First choice was my brother's son Niels Peter, who was Makonnen's age and happy to be included in the project. Then we decided we needed to make the cast multi-racial, so we asked the Chinese proprietor of a store where I bought Makonnen's LEGO toys and, Yes, he had a son who he would allow to participate.

I asked a friend at the US Embassy to help us find a White child, and he introduced me to a nice lady who thought it would be fun for her and her son Chester to have a North Coast vacation with a difference. Now we needed a girl. Makonnen said he had met a pretty little girl named Sky whose father, Carrot Jarret, was a member of the Third World reggae group. We found her at home with her mother Gina, and not only did she agree, but she herself was so beautiful and happy to be around children, that I invited her to play the lead adult role.

By an amazing miracle, also at Sky's home was reggae superstar Freddie McGregor. Makonnen decided to ask this famous man, whom he had never met before but had heard of, to be in his movie. To my great surprise, with a big smile,

Freddie McGregor said Yes.

As I went ahead planning for a long weekend shooting the film, hiring my friend, Rasta television cameraman Ray Smith and Wayne 'Insane' Bowen as production assistant, people said "Don't plan on Freddie McGregor. He's not going to come. He spends every Saturday at the racetrack with his horses." I just waited and hoped that all would be well.

It was. Freddie McGregor turned up and spent the weekend filming with us, even giving a live performance backed by the hotel band, that was a major feature of the film.

Boscobel gave our film team the Penthouse suite overlooking the sea, with 3 bedrooms, sofas, indoor jacuzzi and full access to everywhere on the property. General Manager Geoff McKitty agreed shyly to play himself in the story and the staff were delighted.

The Entertainment Manager had laid on some special events at the hotel while we were filming, including a performance by leading singer Karen Smith that we included in the film. Another good friend was Paul Dadd, Water Sports manager, who gave us his sailing yacht and crew for us to film scenes on the water.

We had a wonderful time filming and I am proud of the half hour film that resulted. I wrote some verses for Makonnen's theme song, we got Wailers producer Tyrone Downie to produce it and Suzanne Couch to sing it, and we hoped it could become a series for Jamaican television and maybe the world. It wasn't the greatest film in the world as the children were not professional actors and this was my first effort at making a 'story' film.

But once again Paul Bucknor the boss at JBC-TV , the only visual broadcaster at the time, turned down the opportunity to show a film of mine.

Undaunted, I entered a copy in the Chicago International Children's Film Festival, and to my surprise the festival invited Makonnen and me to be their guests. Flown to Chicago and treated like celebrities, our film won an Audience Award and Makonnen was hailed as a "Peter Pan".

I used the trip to link up with two sets of friends we had in Chicago, and after the festival ended we spent some time in that interesting city.

*

With such success on the first effort, I looked for an opportunity to make a sequel. Two years later, Makonnen and I were on one of those around-Jamaica journeys that take place when visiting family and spacious beaches houses dotted around the island cause a convoy of vehicles filled with happy people, clothes, food and music to hit the road and enjoy Beautiful Jamaica for a while.

This special journey took us from the cool hills of St Andrew to the white sand beaches of Duncans, before coming to a stop in Negril, where Makonnen and I were delighted to meet the Saulter family. Greer-Ann and Bertram were upper-class Jamaicans who had dropped out of St. Andrew life to live a semi-hippy, semi-Rasta life in Negril. They had built a garden home on the Lighthouse road, opened a natural restaurant and were raising 5 children in an idyllic lifestyle while turning a cliffside spot into a cut-stone and thatched roof hotel.

The children Storm and Nile, were boys Makonnen's age. There was also Astro – who had cerebral palsy and used a computer as brilliantly as Stephen Hawking, and Shasta – a very beautiful young girl with curly golden hair, golden skin color and a golden smile.

"Mom," said Makonnen as soon as he saw her: "Let's make a movie with Shasta."

It seemed like a good idea. As the families sat around one evening enjoying the peace and naturality of the Saulters' home and each other, we showed the first *"Kids Paradise"* and talked about making a sequel. The boys were happy with the idea of doing something as interesting as making a film. They grew up around film people like Perry Henzell, so being in a film would be something interesting to do in the cultural backwater of Negril. Shasta agreed shyly.

The Saulter parents were fine with the idea, so we went back to Kingston and set up the second film. The story would be that Makonnen and his cousin were vacationing again at the same children's hotel, when they meet Storm, Nile and Shasta, who is now a fashion model and hating the job. She runs away from the hotel, Mak and the boys go look for her and find her. As a reward, Storm and Nile invite Mak and Peter to Negril, where they have another adventure catching coral thieves.

As well as the children, the film's stars were Elise Kelly who played Mak's Auntie, Judy Mowatt as herself performing at the hotel, Cayman singer Jean-Eric 'Natch' Smith, and Jamaican hotel executives Peter Fraser and David Ellis.

We filmed at the Jamaica Grande in Ocho Rios as our first hotel, and another location was the beautiful dining room situated over the swimming pool at Ernie Smatt's seaside mansion. From Ocho Rios we moved to The Caves, the Saulter's cliffside hotel in Negril that was just opening up at the time, but which has now become the most exclusive Negril resort. There's a fashion show in the film, a sea chase and Rasta dancing and drumming by JAH Chilren, Patsy Ricketts talented family.

The film was well acted, as the children were older now. But the lack of success of my second film did not rest in our artistic and creative abilities, but in economic mistakes. I had persuaded a leading businessman to invest in the film's potential and own a major percentage of the royalties. He agreed to the investment by insisting that the funds not be deposited in my hands, but in the account of someone he trusted. My businesman brother Peter was selected.

Peter then insisted on hiring a friend of his as film crew, a man with neither experience nor reputation, but who I later realised owed Peter a debt that was repaid by him doing this job for little or nothing. This meant I had no power to hire or fire crew, as I was merely an unpaid employee.

On the first chaotic day of filming, when none of the eight persons hired seemed to know what to do and yet none would take instructions from me, I asked to be shown the day's rushes. I was told that they had no equipment to show the footage. It was unthinkable that a film production should be unable to review its work as it is made. This is where I should have fired them and hired a new crew, but I had no power. Each day's work was a tragedy of poorly-recorded sound, confused crew, edgy children and a bitter experience for me.

Thankfully, I was able to piece together and edit a completed film, but I keep thinking how much better it would have been if I had been able to make it with the same 3-man crew I used for the first *Kids Paradise*. This episode did not make it to the Jamaican TV screen either, but one day I will upload them both to YouTube for those interested to see them.

The interesting part of this story, though, it that both Storm and Nile went on to become leading Jamaican film makers after being part of *Kids Paradise 2*. They were sent to study film making in the USA under acclaimed film makers and are now acknowledged as Jamaica's best young film makers. I can smile when I see the good work my humble efforts inspired.

*

My third film came from Makonnen's appointment as Youth Technology Consultant to the Government just as the world was opening up to the miraculous uses of technology, especially the spread of the internet. Everyone wanted to learn how to build a website and email made it so easy to communicate with people all over the world. Individuals and businesses were set up to teach technology and help guide individuals around the worlds of Microsoft and Apple.

I thought it would be a good idea to make a half-hour TV programme on technology hosted by Makonnen that would have features, news and interviews. Carl Bradshaw, the actor, thought it was a good idea too, so he brought us into Island Records offices in New Kingston to put it together.

We got word from Melissa Sconyers, the bright homeschooled techie with whom Makonnen had won the Think Quest website award in Hollywood, that she and her mother were coming to Jamaica on a cruise ship with a brief stop in Ocho Rios. We thought an interview with Melissa would be a great feature of the programme, so we arranged to meet her in Ocho Rios and film an interview at Golden Eye, the beautiful resort owned by Island's boss Chris Blackwell.

Having the freedom of Jamaica's nicest resort at our disposal, we gave Melissa and her mother the luxury of a beautifully-appointed cottage, a well-prepared meal, jet-ski rides over the lagoon to James Bond Beach and a swim in the Golden Eye pool, while we filmed the interview inside the house where Ian Fleming wrote the Bond books.

A segment of the programme was an interview with 10-year-old Indongo Davis, a bright youth who as a Techschool Jamaica student had build his first website and was happy to describe how he did it.

After Melissa and her mother returned to continue their cruise, we returned to Kingston and added some tech information news, an experimental animated film and wrapped up the half-hour show.

Once again TVJ didn't consider my work worthy of broadcast on their station.

*

The Road Through the Blue Mountains of Jamaica is my classic documetary film.   I have lived in many places thanks to the kind human heart of good people rescuing me from homelessness.

One such time was when we lived in the Blue Mountains countryside. Without resources to do otherwise, I had accepted a friend's offer to stay in his unoccupied house high up in the coffee slopes above Kingston. It was a very remote location, accessible only by packed country bus departing from Papine in the evenings and crowded taxis heading down off the hill in the early mornings, as we had no car.

It was difficult living there and getting to and fro. However, the one advantage was that the road had just been upgraded through a contract between Government and the European Union, so the surface was smooth all the way up. Along the way the road passed through the most beautiful garden scenery to be seen in Jamaica, flowers and trees of all kinds on the ground, on branches, as orchids, as coffee blossoms, as rare tree ferns and giant mahoes. The mountains were themselves a spectacle, often covered in clouds drfting across them like pale white horses. Waterfalls splashed onto the road as we drove past, and everything was washed bright and shining.

I decided that a National Geographic-type film needed to be made about the road through the Blue Mountains, so I decided to try and make it myself for Jamaica. I contacted the CPTC (the government's Creative Production & Training Center), showed them some photos of how beautiful the journey was and persuaded them to give me the equipment and editing services to do a co-production with me as producer.

I am proud of the beauty that this film has captured for posterity, especially now the Blue and John Crow Mountains have been named a UNESCO Heritage Site. The scenery will change over time, but my film is a record of the Road at its most beautiful, and the people who made it beautiful.

*

I made a good short movie when trying to get a film version of my novel *'Joseph – a Rasta Reggae Fable"* made with a 5-minute trailer of scenes featuring Carl Davis, Earl 'China' Smith , Makonen and (surprise!)Lennox Lewis. When after ten years it hadn't inspired a producer, someone told me that a very powerful person stops every effort to make a 'story' film about Bob Marley (and there have been many efforts, I was told). If only I had known, I would have saved myself a lot of effort and money long ago.

Other films I have made include documentaries-for-hire, the most memorable one covering a 10-day summer retreat for 20 young Caribbean singers, musicians and producers run by Lloyd Stanbury for UNESCO. I not only filmed the many activities on the schedule, but also edited it each night into a finished film that was shown a week after the retreat ended. Quite a marathon job!

I have also worked on other people's films, including making a film of the filming of the Jamaican feature film *'KLA$H'* with Giancarlo Esposito and Jasmine Guy, and as Jamaican liaison for an Irish TV film crew making a documentary about reggae.

I keep trying to make more films, so this list may grow.

THE REGGAE FILM FESTIVAL

In 2007 Peter Gittins, an English reggae and film enthusiast, contacted me to ask if he could include my film *'Race, Rhetoric, Rastafari'* in a database of 'reggae films'. I was surprised to learn there was such a genre of films, but he informed me that Jamaica's reggae music has influenced a lot of film makers to document aspects of the culture and people who made it, as well as to make films with reggae soundtracks. His contact inspired us both to launch an annual series of Reggae Film Festivals from 2008 to 2013 showcasing the films and Jamaican culture.

Thus came the catalyst for my revival as a film festival organizer, when Peter Gittins started collecting all the films he could find that featured reggae in some way, whether as soundtrack or as documentary subject. He found there were scores of films, mostly made by non-Jamaican lovers of reggae and including several feature films and excellent documentaries. With a collection of the best of these showing the potential, he persuaded me to use my film festival organizing skills to produce a festival of reggae-themed films.

In 2007 while working again with Babsy Grange, then Minister of Culture, I persuaded her to include a Reggae film Festival in the first Reggae Month and with the help of several sponsors, the first Reggae Film Festival took place at on February 22, 2008 at Emancipation Park under a full moon eclipse.

The impact of the Reggae Film Festival went beyond the event's success and the good vibe it generated in the local film industry. News of the Festival travelled to all the countries whose films were represented. These included Germany's endearing feature film *'Almost Heaven'* ; the amusing Rasta road trip *'Roots Time'* from Argentinia; Jep Jorba of Spain's reggae biography of *'Rico Rodriques – The Legend'*; the USA/JA collaborations of *'KLA$H'* with Bill Parker and *'Ernie Ranglin: Roots of Reggae'* from Arthur Gorson, and films from Canada and the UK, as well as the Jamaican films *'Countryman'* and *'Stepping Razor – Red X'* by the brothers Dickie and Wayne Jobson.

Blogs, websites and magazines on reggae picked up the story, many publishing articles about the films and film makers, generating interest in Jamaican film making. Almost overnight, the world woke up to the fact that Jamaica's reggae music has inspired a new genre of films that have earned their own classification. The film makers may have been born here or there, but what has inspired them has been the heartbeat music of Jamaica's reggae.

In 2009 I went on my own to produce the second Reggae Film Festival, presenting films at the government Creative Production & Training Center (CPTC). In 2010 the film festival was held at the Sheraton Kingston Hotel, at

which we inaugurated the Make A Film in 24 Hours
competition that went on to reveal the hidden talents of
many new, young Jamaican flm makers. Entrants were given
a theme word on the first day of the Festival to make a 5-
minute film and return it in 24 hours. The 2010 winner, *"At
the Supermarket"* by Jay Will, is still a perennial delight
wherever and whenever it is shown, and the entry by Craig
"Amaziah The Great' Kirkland showed the world his amazing
and untutored film making talent. Other film makers who
entered films the competition were Adjani Salmon, Basil
Jones Jr., Christopher Byfield and Vanessa Phillips.

2010 was the year in which the talent of Kurt Riley
was revealed. Kurt started making music videos in 2008 with
an amateur camera he had been given, and decided to make a
feature film. The result was *"Concrete Jungle – Kingston 12"*,
a revealing story set in Kingston's ghetto that won the Best
Feature Film award. Kurt has since gone on to make other
feature films and is now recognized as a leading young
Jamaican film maker. We also showed Ginger Knight's film
of his play *"Room For Rent"* that had successfully been
transformed from stage to screen.

We moved the event to the Pulse Entertainment
Center in 2011, where the cricket documentary *"Fire In
Babylon"* won the Best Documentary award over *"Holding
on to JAH"*, and actress Esther Anderson premiered her film
"Bob Marley – Making of a Legend" with rare footage of the
singer early in his career when his locks were just starting to

grow. "*Rocksteady*" the American feature film about a race-car driver co-starring reggae artist David 'Steel Pulse' Hinds, won the Best Feature Film award and Reinardo Chang showed his amazing talent with his innovative dancehall-inspired '*Dutty Bwoy*' cartoons to win the Digicel Animation award. Other animators whose work came to light in the Reggae Film Festival were Corretta Singer, Stephen Williamson and Kevin Jackson, who started the growth of a Jamaican animation industry.

In 2012 we had the benefit of a sponsor and presented the film festival on the poolside lawns of the prestigious Jamaica Pegasus Hotel. Our opening night film was attended by the US Ambassador Pamela Bridgewater and Jamaican Ambassador Aloun Ndombet Assamba, who viewed Harry Belafonte's documentary "*Sing Your Song*", among other notable films. Sad to say, the Marley empire thought Reggae Film Festival week was a good time to screen their commissioned documentary "*Marley*" and without involving us in any way, took over the Emancipation Park across the street from the hotel for a massive premiere held on the second night of our event.

Million$ were spent to transform the Park into a cinema for thousands, with giant screens all around and even a Red, Gold and Green carpet for VIPs to walk on, which aroused the anger of the Rastafari community and had to be removed. I was disappointed, but continued the week's Reggae Film Festival events, presenting Chris Browne with a

Lifetime Achievement Award for his years of film-making work.

In 2013 we moved the event to Ocho Rios, where another favour from my friend Chris Blackwell gave us his beautiful Island Village with its big stage and spacious lawn surrounded by boutiques and cafes. The 2013 year's theme was Women In Film, honouring Jamaican film actress Madge Sinclair who came to public attention in the Eddie Murphy film *"Coming to America"*, along with Grace Jones, Bond girls Marguerite Lewars and Martine Beswick, stage and screen actress Leonie Forbes and Tessa Prendergast who not only acted in some minor Hollywood films, but was noted as the designer of the famous white bikini worn by Ursula Andress in *"Doctor No"*.

Several awards in 2013 went to women, including '*Hill & Gully*' by Jamaican-American director Patrice Johnson for Best International Feature, the award for Best Jamaican Feature going to director Judith Faloon-Reid for '*Just Another Friday*", while the Short Feature award was presented to UK TV series '*Dear Jesus*' by Danielle Scott-Haughton, with an Honour Award for '*One Song*" a short feature from Austria by Catalina Molina.

The Best Documentary Award went to *"Born in Trenchtown"* by Greg Pond that gave the history of Kingston's controversial ghetto, while a special Honour Documentary

Award went to *"Akwntu – The Journey"*, a view of Maroon country by Ja-American director Roy Anderson. There was also an award for Reggae History, won by '*Keeper of Zion Gate*" and presentation of a Music Video Award to Costa Rican group Mystica, while the Comedy Feature award film *"Lost in Dangria"* from Belize had the audience in stitches with its amusing story.

But with lack of ongoing financial support, I decided to stop trying to hold another Reggae Film Festival. Looking back, I am proud of the achievement as I see that the event has opened the public's eyes to the vast amount of cinematic attention being paid to Jamaica's music culture. In the years since the first Reggae Film Festival, several Reggae films have been completed or are in production, and many have been welcomed by the Reggae film circuit. Best of all have been the many opportunities the event gave for Jamaican film makers to expose their talent for the first time to a Jamaican audience.

My big mistake with the Reggae Film Festival was that it made no money because instead of thinking people would pay money to see the films, which no one did, instead I should have charged the film makers money to show their films. Being in the flm festival enabled them all to do so much with their films, and I would definitely have earned some money, instead of finding myself totally penniless after giving up in 2013.

But to look for the silver lining, the Reggae Film Festival will rest in history as one of the many projects I attempted to make my beloved home a greater, better place.

DAWTA OF JAH:
A Spiritual Journey Into Rastafari

*Speech to the Texas Christian University Honors Convocation.
April 7, 2016*

"I am because we are, and because we are, therefore I am."

Truly, the mutuality and community reflected in this elegant African proverb is fulfilled in your hearing today. My beloved son, Makonnen, and I would not be here with you this morning were it not for the generous support and gracious hospitality of so many connected with the Provost's Office, TCU's Honors College, Professor of Religion Darren Middleton and various faculty as well as staff associated with TCU's Discovering Global Citizenship program.

After 86 short but turbulent years, RASTA has come in from the cold, as Bob Marley predicted it would, and I appreciate your invitation to outline how.

The RastafarI movement grew out of the darkest depression that the descendants of African slaves in Jamaica have ever lived in -- the stink and crumbling shacks of zinc and cardboard that the tattered remnants of humanity built on the rotting garbage of the dreadful Dungle community on Kingston's waterfront. Out of this filth and slime arose a sentiment so pure, so without anger, so full of love, the Philosophy of the RastafarI faith. It was a flower in a pigsty, watered by the nourishment of the Prophet Marcus Garvey, swayed by the wind of local political activism, and cherished by the Black man's long-withheld desire to hold his head upright. Freedom of Spirit, Freedom from Slavery and Freedom of Africa, was its cry.

HAIL! JAH RASTAFARI!

2016 is the International Year of Rastafari, in which RASTA celebrates the 50th anniversary of the historic visit of Emperor Haile Selassie I to Jamaica. I stand before you as a RASTAFARI CHRISTian, a member of a new interpretation of CHRISTianity that, controversial as this may be, is in fact a reality. Yes, I am a CHRISTian, a believer in Jesus of Nazareth who achieved the crown of CHRISThood. It's a new and BLACK form of CHRISTianity and I will be happy to tell you what it is and how it has shaped my spiritual journey.

I was baptized a Roman Catholic at birth, confirmed an Anglican at boarding school aged 14, and stepped forward to be "saved" by Billy Graham aged 17. Between the years 17 to 30 I lived a conventional Christian life, going to church less and less often as I moved from Jamaica to live in England, but still upholding the Christian traditions, rules and commandments I had been brought up with. This heritage taught me that Christ was the Son of God, the unique and perfect man who died on the Cross to redeem me from my sins – sins which I had already committed and other new ones that I would undoubtedly commit, as I was only human and imperfect. Only Jesus Christ was perfect, of all the humans who had ever lived on earth. I had the typical Christian inferiority complex – only one human had ever been PERFECT and I therefore had to live with and accept my deficiency and subsidiarity.

This attitude of inferiority was easy to accept, because I had been raised as a typical Jamaican of colour in a country where 90% of the population was associated with and descended from enslavement of African people by European colonizers whose right to be rulers was automatically accepted even after slavery and colonization had ended. I had readily accepted my supposed second-class status because I had been taught by life, school, even parents, that everything of European origin was instantly and rightly better than anything of African descent, that Africans had been enslaved because Africans were a substandard race that could only be helped by becoming as European as possible. After all, Jesus Christ was European, wasn't he?

I lived with that mental slavery until my mid-20s, when I moved to live in England and to live with the endemic racism that we brown-skinned Caribbean immigrants experienced from the native English people. It was singularly unpleasant to live with such relentless hatred, but we knew what to expect because we had been brought up to believe in our racial inferiority.

But a lot of racial and social bubbles were burst internationally by the Swinging Sixties, the Black Power Movement, the flower-power hippies and the US anti-Vietnam-War movement, whose young White-skinned people forced down the walls of bigotry and discrimination.

Racism is a cruel sword that pierces the heart. It can be fought with anger, guns, revolution like the Black

Panthers. Or it can be fought with knowledge, education and pride in one's ancestry. That's the choice revealed to me when I saw Perry Henzell's 1972 film, *'The Harder They Come'* which introduced me to a Jamaica I did not know: the Jamaica of the voiceless and marginalized, the Jamaica of indigent communities with names such as Trench Town, Back-O-Wall, and Dungle, the Jamaica of RASTA.

There, amid the language of my Jamaican people and the rhythms of reggae, I found pride in my African history and heritage.

Perry's film epitomized the social changes taking place in the early 1970s. The scene of a RASTAman shaking his locks as he rose from the Caribbean sea changed me from being and thinking like a brown-skinned Englishwoman, and started me on the road whose destination became RASTA for I. I left the bitter cold of English racism and fled to the warm shores of my homeland Jamaica to begin my education.

The distance from the earliest RASTAs who hid in hillside encampments to avoid brutality from police and who withdrew from a society that scorned them as blasphemers, criminals and madmen, to me – an educated, renowned RASTAwoman who once served as a Senator in my country's Parliament – is only 8 decades, almost as many years as I have been on the planet. As you say in Texas, "Who-da-thunk-it?"

I have tried to think it through. My books and articles have recorded the Rastafari movement's arduous journey from those early days in Leonard Howell's Pinnacle commune to the violent incident of Coral Gardens in the Montego Bay area in 1963. Also, I have taken my own tour of duty as a Jamaican Senator and my global experience as a RASTA to folk in Jamaica and elsewhere, including stops in Fidel Castro's Cuba, the Cold War's East Germany and Saddam Hussein's Iraq.

But my most important teacher was Marcus Mosiah Garvey, the Jamaican philosopher who embodied as well as preached a message of black somebodiness and African excellence. A brilliant orator, Garvey's most important and most memorable statement was this:

"If the White man has the idea of a White God, let him worship his God as he desires. If the yellow man's God is of his race let him worship his God as he sees fit. We, as Negroes, have found a new ideal. Whilst our God has no color, yet since the white people have seen their God through White spectacles, we have only now started out to see our God through our own spectacles. The God of Isaac and the God of Jacob let Him exist for the race that believes in the God of Isaac and the God of Jacob. We Negroes believe in the God of Ethiopia'"

Garvey's Pan-African message influenced the start of the Universal Negro Improvement Association. Although its members were mostly descendants of slaves in the United States, the UNIA influenced some Jamaican men who were struggling to survive the debilitating effect of slavery and colonialism at home by thinking their way out of their condition and trying to find a new philosophy that would fit their condition and their desire to be equal with all others.

These were the first RASTA thinkers, charismatic street preachers such as Leonard Howell, Archibald Dunkley and Joseph Hibbert. The men they influenced became the first generation of RASTA, the hermits and sages who moved from the towns into the hillside encampments where they reasoned on Garvey's racial philosophy, studied world history and read their Bibles. These were the teachers whose student I became and they included some of the faith's founding Elders such as Douglas Mack and Sam Clayton, who in 1961 went on the first Mission to Africa to explore the concept of Repatriation.

RASTA was a home-grown Jamaican philosophy that reached beyond Africa to the specifics of Jamaica and Jamaican culture that had been brought from Africa and mixed with Europe into a homogenous whole in which different shades of skin colour were united by one indigenous mindset.

My faith as a RASTA grew alongside the international outreach of RASTA Reggae and in company with many of the musicians taking the RASTA message to the world in their songs, most especially Bob Marley, who was my friend from 1972 until his passing in 1981.

I used to stop by his house at 56 Hope Road on my way home from my job in the Office of the Prime Minister just down the road, and I would sit in the backyard listening as he and his friends made music, laughed and talked about Rasta; or I would watch them play football, "proper football,".

Sometimes I got a chance to sit in the studio while he recorded songs like "*I'm A Black Survivor*".

The growing global acceptance of Marley's music and life gave confidence to the faithful that our belief was not incorrect, if the world so eagerly and happily accepted him and what he represented. Most of all, this global acceptance of Marley caused public opinion in Jamaica of RASTA to change, especially because of the wealth he earned.

BOB MARLEY was the Psalmist of the RASTA Reggae generation and his songs taught that RASTA's messages were not limited to Jamaican people alone, but resonated around the world. Think of the lyrics to "*Three Little Birds*"; to "*Coming In From The Cold*"; to "*Get Up Stand Up*", which was sung as the Berlin Wall was being brought down in 1989. And, think of "*One Love*", the global anthem of transglobal, transcultural humanity. For me, as for so many RASTA, Marley's songs constitute an unofficial Rasta hymn book.

April 1966 represented a pivotal moment for RastafarI. In 1966, His Imperial Majesty Haile Selassie I visited Jamaica. The Emperor responded to the publicity and the overwhelmingly warm reception he received with gratitude and humility, but he was distressed by the thought that Rastas were worshiping him as God.

The Emperor's response to his experience with RASTA in Jamaica can be deduced from statements made by him through Abuna Yesehaq, his personal priest whom the Emperor sent to establish the Ethiopian Orthodox Church in Jamaica in 1970. In an interview I conducted with him,

Abuna Yesehaq quotes the Emperor as saying, concerning Rastas, "I want you to help this people; my heart is broken because of the situation of this people. Help them to find the TRUE God, teach them!"

Abuna Yesehaq was indefatigable in his efforts to establish the EOTC in Jamaica and the Western world, baptizing many RASTA in the Ethiopian Orthodox Christian faith and teaching them the glorious history of the Church, one of the oldest branches on the Christian tree. The presence of the Church reminded critics that RASTA rose from Christian foundations, while at the same time giving RASTA a direct and continuing connection with the Emperor.

Some people are shocked when RASTA presents Ethiopian icons of Christ with brown skin and African features, even dreadlocks, and some are even more shocked to see the Catholic Pope bowing before one of the many icons of a Black Madonna. But it was RASTA that first pointed out to me that if Jesus of Nazareth was a Caucasian European, he would either have had a good suntan to protect him from the desert sun, or else would have had skin cancer. Then we moved to the next step, that of recognizing that Africa is the original Eden, the Promised Land, and that black people are the descendants of the ancient Israelites.

When anthropologist Robert Lecky announced that ALL humankind came out of Africa, and in fact out of Ethiopia, the shock echoed around the world and is still being felt.

For, if the first humans started in Ethiopia near Lake

Tana, the source of the Nile River, it can be seen that humanity flowed down the Nile from Ethiopia to Egypt where the greatest and most advanced civilization in history existed ---a civilization whose mysteries are still unfathomed!! We are all, indeed, out of Africa! Africa is the cradle of life and Ethiopia is birthplace.

RASTA challenges us to answer questions such as: How will Christ return? Or has Christ already returned in another form – or even as another man? Is Christ the spirit of God, manifested in many people? We don't know, but when we see that one man has been able to inspire millions to follow a way of life described and exemplified in Jesus of Nazareth who achieved the title of Christ, we hold reverence for that man. Some even call him The Christ Returned.

I myself do not call His Imperial Majesty Haile Selassie 'God' or even 'Christ'. That's where I differ from some other Rastas. I call H.I.M. the Divine CHRISTLY human who directed me to God in Christ, who showed me the best example of how to be Christly, how to be a CHRISTian by following the Ethiopian Orthodox way of being and seeing CHRIST. Not all Rastas think this way. But how I think is a powerful testament that MANY profess.

Testimonies like mine have given H.I.M. Emperor Haile Selassie the fame and reputation he holds and even led some of us, myself included, to campaign for his elevation to Sainthood. Muslims have seen God-Allah through Muhammed. Hindus see God through Krishna. Every religion on earth has had a human Avatar.

Selassie is the Avatar of the 20th Century Man of Righteousness, the messenger of JAH, or God's vessel, for whom skin colour is not as important as spiritual correctness, Godliness. By whatever process, that Man, Haile Selassie, has arrived at that BLESSED state of being.

I am a Dawta of JAH. In my 40 years as a RASTA I have been able to use opportunities to speak and write as much and as often as possible to spread the truths and dispel the myths and misconceptions about RASTA. Now that RASTA has its own historians and spokespersons, the faith will be stronger and more easily understood. This is no small virtue. Being a woman is an advantage also.

When I started my spiritual journey, or what we RASTA call "trodding," women had little or no voice, though this eventually changed over time. I was one of the second generation of Rastawomen, grown in recent years as independent womanhood, committed to helping women and men in the Rastafari movement address gender issues together.

We are not where I'd like us to be, I will be honest, but I see today how my prominence and outspoken advocacy of such topics as ganja legalization and Reparations has inspired a younger generation of RASTAwomen to construct their own identities and cultivate their own roles within the movement, while still maintaining the traditional RASTAwoman's role as mother and home-maker.

2016 is the International Year of Rastafari and I am a Dawta of Jah.

Today, I bring you Good News. RASTAFARI is no longer misunderstood and despised. The faith has truly come in from the cold and its "ONE LOVE" philosophy has spread globally as a spiritual belief across all nations and races, with the potential to bring about the much-needed global unification of humanity.

This is the purpose JAH intended for RASTA.

I praise H.I.M. And I thank you.

JAH BLESS.

GROWING UP

After Growing Out in England, I came home to Jamaica and did some Growing Up.

I took the chance to be born again as a new person with a Rastafari mind and spirit and life, a new person, completely different from the person who left Jamaica in 1964, now free from the mental shackles of my origins in slavery and European colonialism.

I have lived a special life as a DAWTA OF JAH, blessed with a rebirth as Rastafari Ethiopian Royalty in a paralell Universe of time and space. We have been the SOUL REBELS in the most HEARTICAL generation the world has known since the ancient Egyptians.

We did not REALLY know but we heard and got the Rasta calling, so we chose to go with the flow and trod that HAAAAAHRDH road, when we could have had the kushy one, but the kushy one is the one which we saw was leading kushy idiots to their DOOM.

They took our Righteousness as folly, so we suffered their slings and arrows in humble patience, while they were forever trying to put us down and consider us inconsequential.

But the times have changed. The sacred Herb they

rejected us for smoking is now legal and they all now want to smoke GANJAH for the inspiration and liberation and healing it brings to body and mind.

That sacred Herb led us to the HOLA Pool of Eternal Life all those years ago in a special Baptism under the Almond trees in the Crystal lights of red, yellow, green, blue, purple, voilet. Many times I sat there in silence and thought I was "seeing" things, but I was seeing the secret light of JAH playing upon those Crystal Hola waters as the sunlight probed through the boughs, branches and leaves to dance the RASTAFARI Secret SPIRIT Dance on the waters and inspire me to sing the RASTAFARI Sacred Songs .... Selah. See I.

So now they want to be like us, to grow their hair in dreadlocks, wear the Royal Red, Gold and Green colours and dance to the Hola Nyahbighi songs. But it can never be the same. We know the real experience, we have lived it through the bitter to the sweet. We can rock and kummmmeeen to the sounds of the magical DUB WIZE with JAH Stone on the turntable rocking the Palace, while minions blow the sacred HERBZ in the faces of those who need to be smoked OUT.

The words are billions, that story is written and can never stop being written, it is like the stars in JAH Universe.

I heave a sigh of relief.

I have finally come home.

Praise H.I.M.

THANK YOU JAH

BLESSED RAS TAFARI

PSALM 19

I will love thee, O Lᴏʀᴅ JAH, my strength.

The Lord JAH is my rock, and my fortress, my deliverer; my God, and my strength, in whom I will trust; my buckler, and the horn of my salvation, and my high tower.

As for JAH, his way is perfect: the word of the Lord JAH is tried: he is a buckler to all those that trust in him.

For who is JAH save the Lord? or who is a rock save our JAH?

It is JAH that girdeth me with strength, and maketh my way perfect.

He maketh my feet like hinds' feet, and setteth me upon my high places.

Thou JAH hast also given me the shield of thy salvation: and thy right hand hath holden me up, and thy gentleness hath made me great.

Thou JAH hast enlarged my steps under me, that my feet did not slip.

Therefore will I give thanks unto thee, O Lord JAH, among the heathen, and sing praises unto thy name.

Great deliverance giveth JAH to his king; and sheweth mercy to his anointed, to David, and to his seed for evermore.

Let the words of my mouth, and the meditation of my heart, be acceptable in thy sight, O JAH.

AMEN

31748019R00152